SPECIAL OF THE DAY

- The pupu platter that exploded . . .
- The Simon Legree tactics—and video spying—of a famous oceanfront eatery
- The chic bistro where a famous actor saved his waitress from an attacking rat
- The guy who insisted on placing his dinner order as a fellow diner succumbed to a heart attack
- The star-studded birthday bash for a famous composer where the cake came in . . . on the carpet
- The complaint that had a crazed restaurant owner running through the dining room with a plate of raw fish

DISCOVER WHAT WAITERS REALLY WANT.
BESIDES THE TIP.

Waiting

BRUCE HENDERSON, at fifteen, was the youngest person ever promoted from busboy to waiter at the Ancestor Restaurant in Stillwater, Oklahoma. After receiving his B.A. from the University of Texas, he came to New York City to become a musician, which has led to numerous gigs— waiting tables.

PLUME
Published by the Penguin Group
Penguin Books USA Inc., 375 Hudson Street
New York, New York 10014, U.S.A.
Penguin Books Ltd, 27 Wrights Lane,
London W8 5TZ, England
Penguin Books Australia Ltd, Ringwood,
Victoria, Australia
Penguin Books Canada Ltd, 10 Alcorn Avenue,
Toronto, Ontario, Canada M4V 3B2
Penguin Books (N.Z.) Ltd, 182-190 Wairau Road,
Auckland 10, New Zealand

Penguin Books Ltd, Registered Offices:
Harmondsworth, Middlesex, England

First published by Plume, an imprint of Dutton Signet,
a division of Penguin Books USA Inc.

First Printing, March, 1995
10 9 8 7 6 5 4 3 2 1

 REGISTERED TRADEMARK—MARCA REGISTRADA

LIBRARY OF CONGRESS CATALOGING-IN-PUBLICATION DATA:
Henderson, Bruce Griffin.
    Waiting / Bruce Griffin Henderson.
        p.   cm.
    ISBN 0-452-27151-7
    1. Waiters. 2. Waitresses. 3. Table service. I. Title.
  TX925.H46   1995
  642'.6—dc20   94–34876
                                                    CIP

Printed in the United States of America
Set in Cheltenham Book
Designed by Leonard Telesca

BOOKS ARE AVAILABLE AT QUANTITY DISCOUNTS WHEN USED TO PROMOTE PRODUCTS OR SERVICES. FOR INFOR-
MATION PLEASE WRITE TO PREMIUM MARKETING DIVISION, PENGUIN BOOKS USA INC., 375 HUDSON STREET, NEW
YORK, NY 10014.

Waiting

Bruce Griffin Henderson

A PLUME BOOK

*To every woman and man
who has ever waited tables for a living*

Acknowledgments

I could not have written this book without the help and support of several people. I cannot hope to repay them in kind, so I would like to thank them by acknowledging their contributions. My agent, Susan Schorr, believed in this project from the beginning and was instrumental in every stage of its development. Christopher Schelling acquired this book at Plume and Peter Borland was kind enough to take it over and do a wonderful job of editing it when Chris left for his new position. I am deeply grateful to both of these men for their guidance and wisdom.

My dear friend Mark Collins listened to me talk about *Waiting* nearly every day for the better part of two years. He let me bore him to tears and gave me invaluable advice in return.

My friend and mentor, William Hauptman, asked me, "Are you sure you want to write a book? It's an awful lot of work." Not only was he right, but he answered any question I had along the way.

Ava Carlotta typed the initial proposal for the book.

Francesca Restrepo read an early version of the book, did

a beautiful design of the manuscript, and has always been as good a friend as I could ever hope for.

In my travels I depended on some of my best friends for shelter. Susan Davison put me up (and put up with me) in Phoenix, Arizona. Maryanne and Kevin Contreras let me stay at their house in Los Angeles and provided me with a West Coast office. Dickie Mallison was a most gracious host in San Francisco. I can highly recommend the accommodations and hospitality at these people's homes.

My family has always been supportive of my creative endeavors. I am very fortunate in that regard. I would like to thank them by name: H. James and Jane T. Henderson, Gretchen and Jeff Denum, Joan Henderson and Ralph Williams, Alissa and Scott Treamer—thank you.

Finally, special thanks to all the good people at Jethro's Bar & Grill, and to every waiter and waitress who sat for an interview.

Bruce Griffin Henderson
August 1994

Contents

I know there's a heaven 'cause I served my time in hell.

—From the back of a Korean War veteran's jacket

Introduction

It was a time of beauty and a time of sadness. It was a time of soft music and late-night suppers in elegant restaurants. There was candlelight and expensive champagne. Love was in the air. It was all so very glamorous. And I was the waiter.

The act of carrying food from the kitchen to a table in a restaurant is, by definition, a service; in the worst cases it can be servile. I should know. For the past eighteen years I have sporadically made my living waiting tables in steak houses, cafes, and continental restaurants. It's not that I intended to make this my life's work; while pursuing a career as a singer/songwriter I have also had jobs driving a gasoline truck, selling French underwear, and working as an usher in a movie theater. But for now, four nights a week you will find me tableside.

If you ask any waiter or waitress why they wait tables you will probably get the short answer: cash. Obviously, anyone who has to work for a living does it to make money, but at the end of a shift, in most restaurants, you walk out the door with a pocketful of cash; and cash comes in handy. If you were to dig a little deeper you might find that most of the people who do this work like to have a flexible work schedule for one reason or another. Many of them are pursuing a career in the arts, or continuing their education; others just don't fit into the nine-to-five world. Some people even wait tables because they like the work.

Of course, waiting tables does have its drawbacks. There is virtually no job security; restaurants open and close as fast as the kitchen door, and restaurant management is notorious for its whimsical nature. There are also no benefits. Most restaurants offer no pension, no health insurance, and no paid vacation time. It goes without saying that there are no paid sick days. If your waiter seems to be coughing a lot, or looks a little green, he probably can't afford to take a day off, or couldn't get anyone to cover his shift. And, yes, we handle food.

The worst part about waiting tables is that you have to wait on people. All any restaurant customer wants is to have everything they want exactly when they want it. That sounds reasonable. But on any given night a waiter or a waitress may have ten or more tables with upward of thirty people in his or her station. At the same moment tables two and eight may want to order, table nine's drinks need to be picked up at the bar, table five needs to be cleared and wants to order dessert, the lady at table four has insisted that you go ask the chef if he will skin, de-head, de-tail, and broil the trout instead of sauté it, and all the while you are stuck on the telephone trying to get an approval for table ten's credit card. It is difficult, stressful work.

I got my first job waiting tables when I was fifteen years old. It was at a steak house called The Ancestor Restaurant in Stillwater, Oklahoma. It was a fairly typical restaurant; the owner was a hard-drinking slave master, the chefs were crazy, we worked eight to ten hours on our feet without a break, and it was a lot of laughs. I learned many important things at that restaurant. Among them were that I could make a good amount of money in a short period of time waiting tables, that most waiters and waitresses are smart and funny, and that a restaurant is a stage for all manner of human folly.

I have an illustrative anecdote. The Ancestor had a bar (which was illegal at the time in Oklahoma) and three dining rooms—the main room, which seated about thirty-five people, and two side rooms, which were fairly private and had five tables in each. One night I had the front room, which was called the Parlor, as my station. The restaurant opened at five o'clock and at about six o'clock the owner told me to come to the bar and take a lone man's order. The man ordered steak and mashed potatoes, and I turned the order in to the kitchen while he made his way over to a table in my station. When I went into the Parlor to ask if he would like something to drink, I noticed that the man was now apparently very drunk. Sometimes guests are like that; they look fine when you serve them a drink, but that one reacts poorly with the ten they had before they came through the front door. I suggested a cup of coffee and he slurred something that sounded like agreement. On the way to the kitchen the owner pulled me aside and told me, "Feed the guy and get his money," because he was plowed. In the kitchen I saw that his food was ready, so I put his plate and the coffee on a tray and served it all at once. It is my custom to wait a few minutes until the guest has had a chance to taste his food and then go by the table to see that everything is all right. Since he was my only table, I returned to the kitchen and was killing some time wiping down the coffee machine when another waiter, Rob Carpenter, came through the swinging doors laughing uncontrollably. I asked him what was so funny, and Rob said, "I think your man wants to talk to you about his meat." Not knowing what to expect, I braced myself and hurried out into the dining room. As I turned the corner into the Parlor I see that my guest, rather than enjoying his steak, has lowered his pants to his ankles and is urinating all around the luxuriously carpeted room. I did the rational thing; I went and got the manager. The manager explained, in no uncertain terms, that the man had to put his pants back on. I cleared the table, wrapped his food, and totaled his check. If I had any doubts about his level of intoxication, they were dispelled when I presented the check. The total was a little over $12. He gave me a twenty and told me to keep the change. It was a windfall, an unheard-of tip for a waiter in Stillwater, Oklahoma, in 1975. The owner and the manager, having parted this man from twelve of his dollars, helped him out to his car and watched him drive away.

Of course, that was an extraordinary event. But something extraordinary happens almost every night in a restaurant. At that job alone I would routinely see people propose marriage, cheat on their wives and husbands, split up, make deals, and dissolve partnerships. Not to mention the poker game that would take place every couple of weeks, where the most powerful men in town would be gathered around my boss's desk eating steak, drinking whiskey, and wagering thousands of dollars on a hand of cards.

Ironically, practically every book I have ever seen about restaurants is about food and the chefs who prepare it. I love food, but it's just, well, food. All of the interesting stuff that happens in a restaurant happens out front in the dining room. It's called *life*. And waiters and waitresses are witnesses to, and participants in, this rich pageant.

This book is about waiting tables. I hope that the reader, if he or she has never done this kind of work, will get a sense of what the job is really like; what is involved in serving food to people in a restaurant, and how hard it is on the mind and body. More important, this book is about waiters and waitresses; the men and women who make sure that you get the dressing on the side of your salad, and serve it with a smile, even when their feet are aching and they don't feel much like being friendly. It is about their hopes and aspirations, and how they *really* feel about bringing that dressing on the side.

To write this book I drove thousands of miles and interviewed many people. I walked into restaurants and asked men and women I had never met to tell me about their work and about their lives. Almost every person I asked sat down and gave me their time and their stories. For this I am very grateful.

The Guests

A restaurant's clientele is its lifeblood. In the simplest terms, if a restaurant has no customers it goes out of business. There are many important factors to developing and maintaining a clientele. A good location is paramount—if they can't find you, or if your location is undesirable, no customers will come through your door. For this reason, and to feed off each other's business, restaurants frequently locate near other restaurants. In larger cities you will often find clusters of restaurants that serve a similar type of food, which often reflects the ethnic makeup of a neighborhood, or which have a similar price range. In smaller towns and suburbs there is often a strip of fast-food and chain restaurants. This can be very disorienting for the traveler. If you pull off the highway in Anytown, U.S.A., and are confronted with a McDonald's, a Burger King, a Pizza Hut, a Denny's, and a Wendy's, the likelihood that you will be able to guess what state you are in, much less get a nutritious meal, is slim indeed.

The food a restaurant serves is also an important factor in attracting customers. If you hope to run a four-star restaurant in Manhattan, you had better serve the best quality food that money can buy and prepare it in an extraordinary fashion (you should also pray that Ruth Reichl likes it). Conversely, if you run a fast-food franchise or hope to compete with one, your food should have plenty of salt and fat and not resemble food in its natural state in any way. It is vital to know what your clientele wants and expects.

The ambience of a restaurant is also critically important. People come to a restaurant to entertain friends and to be entertained as much as to eat, so a restaurant's environment can be as important as the food. It is not uncommon for a chic restaurant in a large city to cost millions of dollars to open. And who knows how much market research was done by McDonald's to discover that its clientele wants to sit under bright lights in molded plastic chairs that are bolted to the floor? The point is that a restaurant, with its food, atmosphere, and service, works to create a pleasurable experience that will make people want to come back again and again. Perhaps the single most important factor in creating this experience is service.

There are three styles of restaurant service: French service, which is when the food is served from a gueridon (a wagon) to the guests' plates in the dining room using a serving spoon and a serving fork; Russian service, which is when the roasts are carved in the dining room and individual portions are served from service platters using a serving fork and spoon; and American service, which is when guests' plates come from the kitchen and are served from the left side with the left hand, and cleared from the right side with the right hand. Not too surprisingly, American service is, by far, the most common type of service used in restaurants in the United States. But these are technical terms. Most people think of restaurant service in terms of the pace at which they are served (did they get everything they wanted when they wanted it) and whether they are treated cordially and with respect. It is the waitstaff who provides this service.

There are three main components to the job of waiting tables: selling food and beverages, delivering food and beverages to the table, and representing the business to the public. Any restaurant consultant will tell you that a waitstaff can make or break a restaurant (the chef or owner will tell you that their unique genius is responsible for any success the restaurant has, but the waitstaff is responsible for any and all failure). Most restaurant customers never have any contact with the chef or the owner, so their impression of how they were treated is created by their interaction with the waitstaff.

The relationship between a waiter and a customer is a fragile and complicated thing. People think of the bartender as being a sort of layman psychologist, but their job is relatively easy—give the drunks their drinks and let them blather; nod appreciatively, commiserate, and laugh. The bottom line is that the bartender has what his clients need and they are grateful. Unfortunately, not as many people are addicted to food, so the waiter's job can be much more challenging.

When people sit down at a table to eat they have very specific expectations. Of course these expectations are seldom articulated, so it is the waiter's job to read the guest's demeanor and to understand the subtext of what people are saying. When a waiter approaches a table he or she must instantly assess what kind of service a customer wants; if they are quiet and reserved or deeply involved with their companion, they will probably want very unobtrusive, formal service. If they are very lively, or loud and boisterous, they might want a different kind of service altogether. If you are jocular with the quiet table you risk disturbing them, and if you are discreet at the loud table they will think you are unfriendly. In either of these situations the guests might believe that they had received "bad service" because their expectations were not met.

In the course of my writing this book, many people who have never waited tables asked me what my book was about. When I told them that it was essentially about waiters' feelings toward their work, these people would invariably tell me a story of how some waiter or waitress had once been very rude to them, or lodge some other complaint about waitpeople in general. A friend's mother-in-law said she was appalled when her dinner companion complained about his shrimp scampi and the waitress asked, "What do you expect this far from the ocean?" (They were in Albuquerque.) My uncle told me it makes him angry when a waitress brings him cold dinner rolls because they're so much better hot. Almost everyone had something bad to say. I would usually get somewhat defensive—after all, I am a waiter, too. I told my uncle that it probably wasn't the waitress's fault that the rolls aren't served hot; in all likelihood the restaurant didn't have a breadwarmer. I told my friend's mother-in-law that there is no excuse for rudeness, but that I wouldn't order seafood unless I could smell the ocean. I felt compelled to defend my colleagues.

As a waiter, I have an idea of what customers think of waitpeople. They think we are rude, they think we're lazy, they think we're trying to cheat them somehow, they think we are purposely keeping their food from being prepared as fast as they want it and in the manner they like it prepared, they think we are always available sexually, and they think we have no feelings. Of course all restaurant customers don't feel this way, but if you wait tables long enough you might begin to believe they do. It is very easy for one bad customer to poison a whole night for a waiter, and by extension, for the few difficult people you are bound to wait on each night to poison your attitude toward customers in general.

I have mixed feelings toward customers. On the one hand, I know that I am dependent upon them—customers directly pay my salary. The more at home I make them feel and the better service I provide, the more money I make. If I do my job well, other factors notwithstanding, people will come back to the restaurant again and again and I will continue to make a living. On the other hand, they sure don't make it easy. People can be terribly rude; they ignore you, they don't say please or thank you, they mumble, they won't look you in the eye, and they say things like, "Gimme a beer," or, "Get me some ketchup." They also do things that are difficult to understand, like come into a restaurant that has no food that they like or can eat, which makes it very hard for a waiter to give them what they want. And like most waiters, I want to give my customers what they want. I take a great deal of pride in my work, and ultimately, if my customers are happy, my work life is much more pleasant.

As I said before, the relationship between a waiter and a customer is a complicated thing. When I examine how I feel about customers I realize that my feelings, too, are complicated. On a bad night at work I might tell you that I hate every person who walks through the door; that they come in exclusively to order me around, make my life hell, speak to me in a condescending way, and think that for an hour and a half they have a servant who can't talk back and who makes them feel like they have control over something in their lives. But most nights I don't feel that way at all. Waiting tables can be a wonderfully social endeavor, and a good restaurant can be a home away from home for the staff and the clientele alike. At every restaurant where I have worked there have been many customers who I can't wait to see again. I have dated people who I waited on, and formed lasting friendships with many others. A good night at a restaurant can make you feel like you are the host of a very successful party, where the guests are a fascinating mix of people you know and people you are meeting for the first time.

I wanted to find out what other waiters and waitresses think about the people they wait on at work. Since the people I interviewed work at a wide variety of restaurants in different cities around the country, I knew that their clienteles would have diverse social and economic backgrounds. I wondered if these factors, and the type of restaurant, might influence the way people behave toward their servers and, hence, the servers' opinion of the customers. I thought of many specific questions to ask, but settled on a very general one: How do you feel about your customers?

There are some days I love being a waitperson because of the interaction with strangers. But there are times, after too much abuse, when I want to spill boiling coffee right over my customer's lap and not even think about apologizing. The regular customers are great, but unfortunately they're all drunks. Tourists are the worst; for some reason they expect New York waitpeople to be nice.

Alexandra Lee
New York City

We'll get a review in *The New York Times* and the management is just nuts for weeks before it comes out. And then people come in and they want to order what is in the review. We change our menu every day, and they might want something that was published in a review a year ago. But sometimes the chef will keep an item on the menu if it was in a review, because he knows people are going to come in and ask for it. The last time Bryan Miller said that the waiters were friendly and helpful. So I had this big table and they had the review out on the table and I could see that they were reading it, so I walked up and I said, "Have you got to the part where it says I'm friendly and helpful yet?" and they said, "Oh, yeah, friendly and helpful."

I don't like most customers. I keep a distance because I feel like I should. I don't like waiters who touch, or are too friendly. But lately one of the things I've been trying to do is be nicer. It's a sort of spiritual thing. I sort of look at it like church—I'm doing a service.

Bob Dombroski
Orso
New York City

The restaurant that I work at, Midnight Lake, is open for lunch and dinner every day of the year except Christmas Day. Lunchtime is mostly businesspeople, and a good percentage of the clientele is Jewish. In the evening the clientele is very gay, being in the heart of Chelsea. It is known for being a gay restaurant. I find the gay clientele to be just as easy or as difficult to wait on as the rest of the population. No matter what you do in life you make assumptions about people, and one of the things I find amusing is that because I work in an ostensibly gay restaurant, many of my customers assume I am gay. One of my favorite stories is about this gay couple I wait on frequently. They are older and very affected. They're sort of like Laurel and Hardy—they give me a hard time but they amuse me. They come in, have a few drinks, give me lots of attitude, and get very drunk. At the end of one night one of them got up to leave and came over to me and said, "How's your lover?" and I said, "Fabulous," and he said, "That's wonderful, wonderful." So I said, "How's yours?" and he turned and looked at his lover, who was sort of peeling himself up from the chair, turned back around and looked me in the eye and said, "My dear, not as good as he used to be."

> Chico Garcia
> Midnight Lake
> New York City

My restaurant is set in the financial district so I have a lot of suits coming in, but then I have a lot of cool people because there are several advertising and architectural firms right around here. So there is a real diversity of people. But what pisses me off about waiting tables is when I go to a table and ask them how they are and greet them and I get no acknowledgment from anyone. That's the thing that bugs me the most. I think that a lot of people look at waiting tables as a demeaning thing. You're there to serve them, so they'll let you know when they're ready. It makes me wish that I could tell them that I'll take care of them when I'm good and ready, but it doesn't work that way.

> Dickie Mallison
> MacArthur Park
> San Francisco, California

I can't stand to be talked down to. I can't stand for people to treat me like I'm a peon. It's funny because some people who go into restaurants are very nice and understanding, if they see that you're swamped they'll say, "We know you're busy," and whatever, but other people act as if they are the President of the United States *and* they're your only table. Because of that I take the opposite extreme when I go out to eat; I'm afraid to ask for anything. It's like, "Excuse me, I swallowed a piece of glass. Don't make a special trip for it, but whenever you get a chance could you please call 911? *Don't go out of your way!* Just whenever you get a chance."

Doug V.
Los Angeles, California

It's amazing how people act in a restaurant. No one who isn't a waiter would even believe it. People aren't aware how stupid they are. When they come in it's like they check their brains at the door. People in this country just don't know how to act in restaurants. I just don't think they have the big picture of how a restaurant works. They don't know what goes into the process of them placing their order and the food ultimately coming out to the table. I don't think they have a realistic idea of what the owner, manager, and waiter can actually give them, and they don't know what they want. In this country people come in and they want to be gone in an hour and a half and not have a miserable time. We don't have free time in this country anymore. So they come in and they are so worried that they are going to have a shitty time and that their whole night will be ruined that they can't enjoy themselves. I keep saying in this country because I lived in Europe and it's not like that over there. When you go out to eat in Europe you don't notice your waiter; he doesn't dictate the kind of time you have. They sit down, and what becomes important is the people around them. They talk; they're not interested in the fact that their friends said this is a great place and that you have to order this or that. They haven't anticipated it for the restaurant's sake. And even if it is their favorite place, every time doesn't have to be like the last time;

they're just there to have a nice time with the people they're with. Here people go to restaurants for warped reasons. They go because it's *the* thing to do. Or they have to date, and they have to take their date to a restaurant. They haven't seen their wife all week because they both work and so they have to take her to a restaurant to see her for two hours. That's a lot of pressure. I don't think it used to be that way.

I think most people see a waiter as someone who is out to foil their best-laid plans. Waiters will tell you that many people come into a restaurant with a chip on their shoulder, or they act like assholes right off the bat. And I think it's because people think that they have to get what they want and need out of a waiter and that's the way to do it. When in reality they should be getting what they want and need out of their lives.

Garrett Harker
San Francisco, California

I find that if you take control of a table, without being manipulative or power hungry, by letting them know that the food is good and the feeling is good, and that you're going to take care of them, then things go okay. In general I would say that 90 to 95 percent of the people I have waited on over the years are good people.

Gary Chiappa
Roettele A.G.
New York City

At Maison Gerard these executives would come in with their little bimbos at lunch, and come back for dinner with their wives. But that was ten years ago, and half those guys are dead now anyway. But the tides don't change, it's just different people filling the shoes. I remember there was this one guy who was a big executive at a movie studio and he walked with a limp. I asked one of the other waitresses why he walked with a limp, and she told me that his wife had found him in bed with another woman and shot him in the balls. There were all these myths about the customers. It became our mission to find out if that one was true. Every time we waited on anybody from that studio we would ask why this guy walked with a limp. They all said his wife had shot him in the balls, so I guess she did.

Holly Gagnier
Los Angeles, California

There are these two older women who are regular customers where I work. They are very dear, in their own way. They are getting older now and they don't come in as often as they used to. But each time these women come in they say, "You got thin dear," or, "You got fat. You look a little fat," or, "Your hair got long. It's too long, you should cut it short like mine." I can see them coming in the door and I think, "I'm going to be too fat this time." It's been going on for years and at this point I'm kind of used to it, but it still makes the hair on the back of my neck stand up because I realize that I have to take this. I have to be pleasant and I have to take it, because that's part of the job. And sometimes that's okay, and sometimes it's really not.

Jennifer
L'acajou
New York City

I often go to bed at night thinking, okay, I'm going to be a good person tomorrow, and then we're going to have a good time next time I work. That's after I come home and realize that I was a bitch. Or else I'll think, let's just assume that every customer is an asshole until they prove otherwise. I think that it is the very consistent stupid behavior of the customers that has made me think like this. On top of all the pressure that we have to work under. I hate to sound anticustomer, but they're stupid. I mean, you go up to a table and say, "Hello, can I get anyone a cocktail?" and nobody will look up or even respond. You get one of three responses: the first and most common is no response at all; they just keep their heads inside the menu. The second one is, "I don't know." And the third one, the one I hate the most, is, "Can we have a few more minutes, *please*?" like you've offended them because you came to the table way too early, but if you waited any longer it would be way too late. All they have to do is go, "We do want a drink, but we don't know what we want, thank you." But there is nothing like that, it happens very rarely. Last night all my tables were so inept. At this one table you could see the anxiety coming over their faces when I asked them what they wanted to drink. I stood there for two minutes, and they just didn't know. Isn't that amazing? They must never go out. And then there's the stupid thing where they say, "What should I have?" to their partner. I don't know what that's about. I may have caught myself saying that one or twice, but ultimately I think I make up my own mind. I think it has to do with wanting attention and blatant insecurity. It's wanting to have what everyone else is having rather than eating what you want to eat. And that tells you everything about that person. That they're watching themselves, they're not being inside themselves. They never really know what's going on inside them when they're in a situation, in any situation; they just want to be what's going on. They don't consider whether they *like* it or not until they get the plate in front of them. I think it is insecurity. You should know what you want. You should know what you want in life; you should know what you want to eat, and if you don't you should think about it and make a decision.

Freeda Kaufman
Jethro's Bar & Grill
New York City

It varies from restaurant to restaurant. Currently I'm working at a three-star restaurant, so you don't get the

Mother's Day crowd—the people who go out to eat once a year and don't know what a fork is. I would have to say that for the most part, the people I wait on are pretty nice. I don't get many difficult customers.

Dan Shapero
San Francisco, California

I think it's funny that we have to call them guests, as if they were guests in our homes. But I sort of feel that I do owe these people something. I mean, they are coming in for a dining experience. They're not here for us, we're here for them; it's that kind of thing. I wish I could have that attitude more often. I'm at the point now where I can barely muster up a smile. Plus, people have requests that I make when I go to a restaurant, but I resent them for it. Like when I ask someone if they want anything to drink, and they just order water. I immediately think, *cheap.* Or if they ask for extra lemon with their iced tea. But I really do think that I owe them a nice time. I *don't* think that I owe them an opportunity to treat me badly. If they're in a bad mood and they're going to be abusive to me, I'd just as soon they stay home. I also don't like to make a lot of small talk; I'm not that kind of waiter. I'm here to serve the food promptly, professionally, and with a good attitude.

Stacey Jurewicz
Pescatore
New York City

The truth? I hate them all. I hate every single one of them. I just don't like needy people. The Ted LoRusso Misanthropic Restaurant. But you'd never know it. I discovered over the years that it was becoming a very unpleasant situation; with the roll of my eyes, or the way I shook my head as I walked away from a table, I was affecting my tips. And not only that, but it was affecting me. I would go home and just be gnarled. So I had to come up with a way to let them know who is in charge, and that they were not going to get the better of me. But I have to allow myself to hate their guts—it's the only way I can survive. I am very nice to them on the surface, but I have little ways of getting my digs in. Instead of, "Thank you very much," I will say, "Fuck you very much," *really fast*. And they never know it.

> Ted LoRusso
> Perretti's
> New York City

When you've got them fed and drunk you've got 'em where you want 'em. With clean ashtrays and full water glasses everything is okay. It doesn't matter what else happens. People never notice when the ashtray is clean, they never notice when the drink glass is full, but as soon as that glass is halfway down, it's, "Waiter! Waiter!"

> Matt Jaroszewicz
> Gainesville, Florida

Customers are pretty cool in general. I don't think anyone likes impatient customers. Foreigners can be hard. Impatient foreigners are the worst.

> Ryan Delmar
> Del's Pizzeria
> Pismo Beach, California

We had a very demanding clientele at Rakel. And the kitchen wasn't the fastest in the world, but they gave good product. It was time consuming—everything was a piece of art. The plate would come out and I'd think, "Gosh, should I hang this on the wall or serve it?" He had an air brush and would spray things like aspic to make beautiful designs on the plate before he put the food on it. So the food would take awhile. But customers would come in and expect food right away. It's the stupidest thing in the world. One Saturday night I was waiting on this party of eight people and the kitchen was slammed. And these were really obnoxious people. Well, the appetizers took about thirty minutes, and the entrées took a while, and this woman and her husband kept bugging me. I mean they would grab my arm—which I hate any customer to do—and say, "Where's the food, where's the food?" and I would say, "I'm sorry, it takes a little while." These were really awful, obnoxious people. And one of the things about this restaurant was at the end of the meal we gave the guests petit fours, really fancy little cakes. So they finished eating and I brought their coffee. But you have to wait for the petit fours because when it's busy somebody else will have the petit-four tray, and the person who makes them makes all the desserts, so she may be busy with that. I ordered a petit-four tray for eight people and I'm at another table taking an order when this lady comes up, grabs my arm and says, "WHERE THE HELL ARE OUR GODDAM CAKES?" right at the table that I was waiting on. Everybody was looking at her like she was insane. I turned to my table and said, "Excuse me, I'll be right back." I went into the kitchen and fixed a petit-four tray myself, took it to them, held it about a foot over the table and said, *"Here are your damn petit fours,"* and dropped it. They jumped all over the place. They paid the bill and she was complaining on the way out, but the manager was unsympathetic because she had been grabbing him every time he walked by also. So I walked up and said, "Don't ever bother coming back to this restaurant, because not one of the waitstaff will serve you." They had left a 10 percent tip on the charge and I scratched it out because I wasn't going to take their money.

Michael Marx
Jethro's Bar and Grill
New York City

People expect the worst of waiters. They really think that you're going to take them. They must think, "We're out here spending our hard-earned money, and we know you're going to trick us." They think you're very lazy and if they don't watch you all the time their food is going to be sitting up there.

Nancy Kelly
New York City

The two worst times to have to deal with somebody is when they are hungry or when they are scared. And the only time that we get to deal with people is when they're hungry. Have you ever noticed how people are when they come into a restaurant? They come in and thirty seconds later they're like, "WHERE'S MY WAIT-RESS?!?" I'm like, "Hello, why don't you sit down first?" And you go over and they're just *mad*. But by the end of the meal they're okay.

Becky Milici
Fama
Santa Monica, California

We have these two people who come in, I think they're a little crazy. They come in all the time and complain and bitch. Half the people who come in here come in to have a bad time and complain and bitch. I guess they just come to get all their shit out.

How do I feel about customers in general? In general they are my tool to make money. You put on a little show for them and they tip you.

Pietro Bottero
The Dock
Fire Island, New York

I found that waiting tables in New York required a certain amount of aggression. I used to say that customers were like children, and we were like teachers. We were going to tell them how they were going to have a good time, we were going to tell them how to behave. And customers responded to that, I found. Out here, you don't tell a customer what they want. The people I work for are from New York and they're always saying, "Go over and tell them this, go tell them that," and it doesn't work out here. In California people want to be asked, and pampered, and treated with kid gloves. It's just not that way in New York.

Monday night we had a premiere party for a new television show. There were 175 people coming for dinner. They were arriving at 6:30 and the show started at 8:00. They wanted a half hour of cocktails and then we were supposed to get them seated, take their orders, and feed them in an hour's time. I have been in the business long enough to know that the people were not going to sit down at 7:00. It's really difficult to get the job done. It's not an office where you are behind closed doors and you can scream and yell and throw papers, you have to remain composed. You have to be calm and in control. I had thirty-five people sit down at ten different tables at one time. And I had to take care of each one of them as if they were my only table, all the while looking fresh, and smiling, and being happy and up. That's where the stress comes in, because you have to swallow it somewhere. You just hold on to it. It's hell. The other thing that is stressful about a night like that is that the people don't seem to trust that I know what I'm doing, and that there is a reason that I am doing everything. That big party had a woman who was the hostess, and she was following me every step of the setup making me move tables. I came up with a floor scheme of where the tables should go, and it was changed three times because she thought something else would be better. And of course by the time the guests arrived the floor plan was exactly as I had originally planned it. Because that was indeed the best way to do it. But they don't trust that waiters know what we're doing, and I don't understand that. I mean, this woman is in television. She doesn't know about the restaurant business, she doesn't know how to make things the most efficient. I'm not going to go to her office and tell her how to produce a television show; why is she telling me how to serve a party?

I like the business. I like waiting on people who are

out to have a good time. I like people who show an interest in what I'm doing. For example, last night I intro-
duced myself to a table and they all remembered my
name, and that made me feel good. I also like the challenge of turning a table around; taking a table that is in a
horrible mood, where the people are out to have a horrible time no matter what happens, and turning them
around so that by the end of the night they've had a
great time. That's my favorite thing to do.

Ray Proscia
Georgia
West Hollywood, California

I have a love/hate relationship with customers.
Sometimes I hate my customers on sight just because
I'm customer-crazy. The worst is when people are just
rude. Somehow, the fact that they leave a tip gives people amnesia when it comes to manners.

Robin Maynor
Linn's Fruit Bin
Cambria, California

One of the reasons that I'm a waitress is that I really
do like people a lot. Of course there are different kinds of
customers. Some people are very relaxed and you feel
comfortable with them right away, and others are very
uptight and you have no interaction with them at all.
And there are different ways of being a good waitress.
One way is to give quiet, good service, where they don't
even know you are there, and another way is to sort of
entertain the customers. You have to know how they
want you to be. And that is something that is intuitive.
It's funny, because the only way to be a good waitress is
to be totally relaxed. I mean, when you go out to eat you
don't think about the waitperson being intimidated by
having to walk up to strangers all night, but it is intimidating in a way. I recently got my friend a job as a waitress. She had worked in catering, but never in a
restaurant. The first couple of nights she was so *nervous*.

And I had completely forgotten about that. Because you get used to it. I think it changes you. It makes you better able to handle yourself in many situations. You learn how to talk to anybody.

Kelsey Geisler
Trompe L'oeil
New York City

I think what this job is about is being a baby-sitter. They always give the tough ones to me. I can handle the sauce on the side and the no salt, no oil, no butter, no cheese. The special orders. And we are in the butt-kissing part of the business at this restaurant. At this restaurant we will do *anything* for a customer. I get the ones no one else can handle, because I can say, "Screw you," in a funny way.

Customers in California are very different from the ones in New York. They're very pretentious, it's very much about the *scene*. But that's this area, too. It's all about the way they look. They have the best boobs on the planet. I mean, the money they spend on their chests is unbelievable. I once waited on a plastic surgeon, and he was adding up how much work had been done on the women in the room; it was incredible. It was much more than the whole restaurant cost to build. It's a trip. I feel like we're the ones with the clue, like we're the only ones who know what's going on. And the gossip is incredible. Now, how this restaurant works, and this is brilliant, is that we have a meeting every night before service starts where the maître d' comes out with the trades. She goes through each customer, if they're *somebody*, and they usually are, and she tells us what movies they've done, who they've slept with, if they're divorced, and what they like on their food. This woman gets paid like you would not believe to know everyone's intimate details. It's incredible. We know more *shit* than most gossip columnists. You can't seat so-and-so on this table because his ex-wife is coming in with her new lover. Or this person is having an affair so we have to get him out because his wife is coming in at 9:30 and she can't see them. It's so insane. It's a circus, and we're pulling the strings. The tabloids call us a lot so we had to sign this agreement that we wouldn't talk to them or we'd lose our jobs. And be sued. So we're not supposed to talk about the customers. A waiter at one of our other restaurants sold the tabloids information and he made a lot of money. Then he got fired.

Robin Shipley
Granita
Malibu, California

I love our customers. They are from all over the U.S. and all over the world. The best part is that they never stay long. We love that.

Rose Larsen
Rose's Den at the Boulder Inn
Milepost 28, Highway 93
Kingman, Arizona

I think customers are what you make of them. If somebody tells me a joke and I go over to a table laughing the people will instantly light up. But I wait on so many tables. There have been nights in my restaurant when I have waited on eighty-three tables; it's the way we work. We have fifteen tables per section and it's wham-bam-thank-you-ma'am. So I deal with a lot of people. I guess it's a microcosm of the world; you can have the nicest person at one table and the biggest asshole that ever walked the face of the earth at the next table. If you let it get to you it's over, you're done. It has to be like water off your back. I try to bring the customers up to where I'm at rather than the reverse.

Tom Andonian
Los Angeles, California

I feel really sorry for customers. It's like they don't know what it's like to be human. And being human is a beautiful thing. I was working in this restaurant in Los Angeles once and my car kept breaking down. You can't be in Los Angeles without a car. So I was riding the bus to work every day, which is like the shame of all shames. It took me two hours to ride the bus to my job. I was working in this place on LaCienega, which is right near Beverly Hills. I was waiting on these two wives, you know, Beverly Hills *wives*. We were talking, and I started talking about my car—how it was broken down, and that I had tried to get it fixed a number of times, and I was really frustrated because I was riding the bus for two hours to and from work every day. So one of these women gets this really great idea and says, "Oh, you should get a new one!" and I was like, oh, thank you so much, I wish *I'd* thought of that. I guess I'll just get my husband to write up a check and get me a BMW. In my best moments I really do feel sorry for them. Because most of the customers I wait on just don't have a clue about what it is to be a *worker*. And, you know, at my worst I just want to drive spikes into their heads.

Waiter X
Khin Khao
New York City

Very Important People

We are all created equal; what happens after that is a dog-gone shame. In a perfect world everyone would be treated the same way regardless of race, creed, appearance, sexual orientation, net worth, or celebrity. Unfortunately, that's just not the case. Walk into Tiffany & Co. in a pair of ragged jeans and a dirty T-shirt and you'll get a feel for what I'm talking about. They might not ask you to leave, but you probably won't get the same kind of attention and service as Donald Trump. Yes, the world is a terribly unfair place. And where better to learn this than a restaurant?

Every restaurant I have ever worked in has given preferential treatment to certain people. In some cases this makes perfect sense; if you have a regular customer who comes in two to three times a week, it pays to keep them happy. I remember being puzzled at my first restaurant job when my boss would buy the rich folks in town dinner or a round of drinks. I knew they could afford to buy what he was giving them. How silly the young are. He wanted their business. Also, since at that time it was illegal to serve liquor by-the-drink in Oklahoma, he needed their influence with the law-enforcement community. One hand washes the other.

In certain cities, a person's social standing can be determined by their ability to book a reservation at a restaurant, or by the table at which they are seated in that restaurant. For some reason, people seem to think that one table is better than another. Except for a particularly loud table near the kitchen, or a breezy one near the front door, I believe that most tables are pretty much equal. But human beings are forever in search of ways to define or declare their status. If a bomb went off in the center of the dining room in Morton's, an upscale Beverly Hills restaurant, on a Monday night at around eight o'clock for instance, the entire entertainment industry would be paralyzed until, like so many Alexander Haigs, the underlings seized control. Could you or I get a table at Morton's on Monday night, much less one in the center of the room? I seriously doubt it. But then again, I don't care. I can't afford to eat at Morton's, and I go to restaurants exclusively to refuel my body. My self-worth does not depend on which table I am seated at, or if the maître d' knows my name. Not everyone feels this way. I read a newspaper article last summer about a fistfight between a restaurant owner and a customer in fashionable East Hampton, New York. The customer was evidently upset about the table at which he was seated. When the restaurant owner told him, "It's the man that makes the table, not the table that makes the man," the customer cold-cocked him. I guess if you're the kind of person who is smart enough to spend $10,000/month for a summer rental that you go to for two days a week, the table you sit at in a restaurant is *very* important.

Television personalities and motion picture actors get the red-carpet treatment in almost all restaurants. This is especially true in Los Angeles, where they are nutty for those thespians. Of course, there is a pretty good reason for this. If your restaurant gets a reputation for being a place where celebrities are found you will get a lot of business in the form of gawkers and hangers-on. That's why you will see maître d's fawning over someone whose last credit was a "Love Boat"

episode in 1977, when they were already a has-been. It's a little different in New York, where the paper tigers of Wall
Street and organized crime figures have celebrity status and
commensurate juice in restaurants. In the Midwest it is different still; there it is the sports figures who reign.

It is all about celebrity, and how important we perceive
people to be. I asked waiters and waitresses to tell me about
the VIPs they had encountered in their work. I was as interested in finding out who they considered to be important people as in the stories they had to tell about them. Here is what
they said.

When you're in New York, once in a while you will
wait on celebrities and it's no big deal. Very low-key.
Here, everything is about show. Especially in Malibu
where they all live in this colony. And we are their Pizza
Hut. They'll call up for a take-out order and it will be
$150. It's this thing where money means nothing. It's just
so disgusting, what they spend on things. Martin Davis,
the president of Paramount, comes in constantly. He'll
come in and sit at this huge table. And he's this big fat
man so we have to bring him this special chair to sit in.
He's the biggest man on the planet; he's *huge*. His wife is
very stiff looking, and she has this ring that is so big that
it has a support that goes under another finger to hold it
up. I swear to God, that's how big this diamond is. And
they have two bodyguards who stand at the door when
they come to eat. Not to guard them—to guard the ring.
It's just so absurd. And they make such a big deal about
everything. I just want to say, "*Hello,* it's *dinner.* We're
talking about food here—*it's no big deal.*" It's really sad.

> Robin Shipley
> Granita
> Malibu, California

At Isabella's you had all the trashy celebrities, the
people you didn't want to see. Rod Stewart would come
in with whatever six-foot-blond Texan model he's with

now; now he's with an Australian, which is the Texan of the British Empire, so it's the same thing. And he would sit there and you could tell he thought we were all just dying, and fighting over who got to wait on him, but we were really fighting over who *had* to. Of course the owner, Steve, was pole vaulting around the place; he had such a hard-on because Rod Stewart was in his restaurant. He was grinning from ear to ear. And there were a lot of wannabes there; everybody wearing what they were supposed to. When I was there it was the little skinny black dress thing; every woman came in with a little black dress. All the men had a little ponytail. And everybody knew what they were supposed to ask, "Do you have a mesquite grill?" And they all knew Steve. When they would hear there was a wait for a table they would say, "Is Steve here?" and I used to want to say to them, "No he's not, and even if he were what would he do, *build* a table for you? The tables are taken, what do you want us to do—kick somebody out?"

Nancy Kelly
New York City

I waited on Raquel Welch once. This was at Rakel, the restaurant. Her husband, who was also her manager, was a nightmare. He was a Class-A American pig. He had on cowboy boots and he had them up on the chair. And the chairs were upholstered! He was a real jerk; he wouldn't even let her order. He was bossing her around at the table, you know, saying have this, have that, and he told me the whole order. I mean, I wanted to hear it from *her.* But she was very sweet.

There was another time when Tim Robbins was in talking to the bartender, Frank. They had gone to school together and he lived nearby, so he would come in a couple of times a week and sit at the bar to chat with Frank. Well, one night the manager, Allison Price, calls Page Six, or one of those columns, and tells them that he's been coming in quite a bit, and the next day it's in the newspaper. Frank got wind that she had planted the story and he told Tim Robbins. He never came back in again, he was so pissed off. Allison was always manipulating celebrities.

Michael Marx
Jethro's Bar & Grill
New York City

At this four-star restaurant I worked at, I started off as the phone bitch. That's what they would call me. There were ten tables in this restaurant, so when we got the four-star review there was literally a three-month wait to get a table. We were booked solid for three months in advance. On the first of every month we would take reservations for the month that was opening up three months ahead. So on the first of every month the phones would be all jammed up. Everybody knew it was hard to get into. In any case, it's not a good idea to call an expensive restaurant and expect to get a table at eight o'clock that night. So one day I answered the phone and this person says, "I would like a reservation for two tonight at eight." This is during the time that we were booked for three months in advance. Holding back the laugh, I said, "I'm really sorry but we're booked for tonight." She said, "But this is a reservation for Mrs. Paul Anka, and it is very important for us to have a reservation for two tonight at eight." I said, "Look, I really can't do it for eight tonight, we're booked up. Maybe I could take your name and if somebody cancels I can give you a call," and she said, "But you don't understand, this is for Mrs. Paul Anka. I really would like this reservation, it's very important. Is there someone else I could talk to?" I said, "No, I'm the only person you can talk to and I'm afraid we don't have anything. But let me just check and see." This was my thing. This is what I would do to calm them down, it was like giving them a Valium. I would put them on hold and do a little work. Now, we would often hold a table for regulars because we only had ten tables to begin with. It was kind of the expensive local hangout for rich artists like Jasper Johns, Merce Cunningham, and Eric Fischl, and it would have been uncool if the local people could never eat there. So we would always try to keep one table aside for a regular, and I had that table but I did not want to give it to this woman. So I put her on hold and talked to my friends for a minute and decided I would give her the table, but I would give it to her at nine. I got back on the line and said, "Listen, I do have a table after all but it's at nine o'clock. Will that be okay?" and she said that would be great, so I said, "Now what was that name again?" and she said, "Mrs. Paul Anka." That's one other pet peeve I have is when people are famous and they use it. It just pisses me off. That whole thing about fame—it's such a bunch of bullshit.

At the peak this place was the *only* restaurant to go to in New York. One night this lady comes through the door in head-to-toe Chanel with her husband. And she's not carrying a purse. That's what I always loved about those type of women; they never carry a purse because they don't pay. And she's all perky and everything. She was from Atlanta, and she said, "Hi, we have a reservation for tonight," and I said, "Great, what's the name?" She gave me the name and I didn't have the reservation. We had a policy that if the customer didn't confirm by three that afternoon we would cancel the reservation. We had to—it was such a small place and it cost so much to keep it open that all the tables had to be full every night. We couldn't afford no-shows. So what I would do when I took a reservation was get their home phone number, or the hotel where they were staying, and try to call them if they hadn't confirmed. And I had tried to call these people at their hotel but they weren't even registered where they told me they would be. Also, I kept really good notes because people would get so hysterical. So I had it together when they came in. Anyway, this lady said, "Well, I made the reservation four months ago on such and such a date, and we're just in here for the weekend so we could come to this restaurant. We came all the way from Atlanta, and I just don't know what I'm going to do if I can't have dinner here!" So I looked at my notes and I said, "Yes, you did have a reservation but you didn't confirm. I specifically asked you to confirm when I took your reservation, and I told you we would cancel your reservation if you didn't. I called the hotel where you told me you would be staying and you weren't even booked there." She said, "We changed our hotel!" and I said, "I really tried to reach you but I couldn't. I'm sorry." And this was the job; you had to say I'm sorry about eight times. I'm sorry. I'm really, really sorry. I'm so sorry. Let me make you a reservation at Montrachet. And by this time she's crying, "I don't want to go to Montrachet!" *Crying!* It's just food, you know? But the thing was, she had to go back to Atlanta and tell her friends that she ate at the best restaurant in America. And now she couldn't do it.

> Freeda Kaufman
> Jethro's Bar & Grill
> New York City

I once waited on Shelley Winters. She came in with three other people, so there were four of them at the table. This was at Spago. They sat down and they ordered a bottle of wine. It was kind of a cheap bottle of wine. I had just opened and poured it when this rich fan of hers said, "Oh, there's Shelley Winters! Send her over a bottle of wine on me," and he ordered a very expensive bottle of wine. So I went over to them and explained that this gentleman wanted to send a bottle of wine to them. So Shelley Winters says, "Is it good stuff?" and I told her it was really good and went to get it. When I got back to the table she was taking the glasses and pouring the cheaper wine back into the bottle. And you *know* that's really hard to do with the tiny hole in a wine bottle. She corked it back up and took it home with her. I loved her, she was great.

Another night at Spago I had Shelley Hack at one table, Tonya Roberts at another table, and Cheryl Ladd at yet another table in my station. Three Charlie's Angels who had all played the same part and gotten fired. And they were all talking about one another.

Maryanne Contreras
Los Angeles, California

Bruce Springsteen used to come in until he and his first wife separated. That was kind of exciting. I always got excited about these people who nobody else has ever heard of. Kathy Acker came in and I got so excited that I overcharged her $10. Louise Bourgeois sometimes comes in, and the first time she came in I couldn't believe it. The other waiters were like, "Who?" I had to bring in *Art In America* and say, "Look! Look! She's really famous. She's really old! It's really exciting!" I used to wait on Jim Jarmusch and Tom Waits when I worked at the Munson Diner years ago. A lot of people who worked there were junkies. I was eighteen and I had no idea. I was always wondering why everyone was so cranky all the time. But all these great people would come in, and I didn't have any idea who they were.

Jennifer
L'acajou
New York City

When I was eighteen I was working at Maison Gerard, which was down the hill from Universal Studios. I was in a ballet company at the time, and Gerard hired almost the whole company to wait tables. He was a really nice man. I did everything there—waited tables, hosted, bussed tables, you name it. And it was a crazy place to work, because at lunchtime everybody would come over from the studio and they had one hour to eat and get back. There were tons of actors and actresses who came in—I remember Robert Wagner and Natalie Wood coming in; I couldn't believe how beautiful she looked. Usually you'd see someone up close and they looked horrible, but she was really beautiful. But these huge stars came in—Barbra Streisand, Natalie Wood, Richard Gere, one person after another. And almost all of them were really nice. And then you'd get the flavor of the season from some TV star who would be a total asshole and you'd want to say to them, "Look, what you're doing isn't that important." It was always the people who were working but weren't really anybody who were the rudest and most obnoxious.

Holly Gagnier
Los Angeles, California

At the place where I work now there are a lot of guests who are supposed to be important, people from the UN, who get VIP treatment and don't treat us very well. But when I worked at Madeleine, on 43rd Street, we used to get a lot of great celebrities. I waited on Eli Wallach and Anne Jackson once, and they were wonderful. They came in and sat down, and for some reason the fire system went off in the kitchen. It covered the whole place with that white stuff, and we had to close the restaurant for lunch. So I had to go up to them and say that I was sorry, but they had to leave. They were so sweet; he held my hand and said, "You're such a dear, we really wanted you to wait on us. We'll come back another time." Many of the celebrities I waited on there were very nice.

Stacey Jurewicz
Pescatore
New York City

I don't really know if it was Cheech, but I once waited on a guy who talked and looked exactly like

Cheech Marin. At the time I thought it was this big hoax on me. He wouldn't show me his driver's license or anything like that, but the woman he was with said he was Cheech. He kept denying it, saying no, no, no. I always wondered about that.

Kelsey Geisler
Trompe L'oeil
New York City

What I like about the business is that you meet so many people. I've waited on so many stars . . . and I have no idea who they are. I was working at this old inn in Nantuckett, it seats thirty people and we would serve 125 people for breakfast. We *turned.* I waited on this table of six and this guy asks the little kid at the table, "Honey, would you like bacon or sausage?" I said, "The kid can't even talk, make up his mind for him." The guy says, "What kind of sausage is it, link or patty?" I told him it was link. He says, "Can you cut the sausage for him?" I said, "It's a tiny link, you take two bites and it's gone—boom, boom." I go in the kitchen and I say, "*Get this!* The guy wants me to cut his sausage for him!" They said, "Do you know who that is?" and I said, "No." They said, "That's Lee Iacocca." I said, "I don't care, let him cut his own sausage." He was a regular customer. Lousy tipper—10 percent.

Becky Milici
Fama
Santa Monica, California

One time, at Chez Pascal, Susan St. James came in. This was a very expensive restaurant, and we would take the guests' coats and hang them in a cloak room. Well, Susan St. James came in wearing this fabulous sable coat with a matching hat. I took the coat, went into the cloak room, and closed the door behind me. Of course, I immediately tried on the coat and hat. So I'm standing there in this beautiful sable outfit when the door suddenly flies open. Who is at the door? Susan St. James. I was mortified. She doesn't miss a beat; she says, "Are my ciga-rettes in there?" I reached in the pocket, got her ciga-rettes out, and gave them to her. She said, "Thank you," and closed the door.

I also waited on Madonna. I was working at a place called The Strand, and it was failing miserably. The owner, Sheila, knew tons of celebrities but she wouldn't bank on it. She wouldn't ask them to come in, and when they did come in anyway, she wouldn't tell the press. We were begging her to do it. One day we were empty, and she said a friend of hers was coming in. She said, "I'm really embarrassed, because we're doing so badly." I told her to relax, that her friend would under-stand. So she's in the back, and Sean Penn and Madonna come in. Then Madonna's family comes in, and the first thing they say is, "We're Madonna's broth-ers and sisters." They ordered their dinner, and I picked the telephone up and it was Cher. So Cher and Chastity came over with Paul Stanley from Kiss. So we have this loaded table, and I said, "Sheila, call the news-papers." Of course, she wouldn't. And it's a shame, be-cause Sean Penn and Madonna's brother were having a contest; they were pulling each other's hair and trying to see who would scream first. It would have made great copy.

Another time, at Chez Pascal, Steven Spielberg came in. He was very quiet and nice. It was a large party, forty people. His people and the people from Atari were celebrating some kind of deal they had just made. It was cocktails and a sit-down dinner. We had a Château Margeaux we were serving for the first course, which was around $75 a bottle. We went through that, and for the main course we had about the same amount of Château Lafite, which was $120 a bottle. I knew we were in trouble; there wasn't enough wine. Sure enough, when the main course was served we filled everyone's glass and we ran out of wine. I went downstairs and told the maître d' that we were out of wine. He told me that he would come upstairs and knock softly on the wall. When he did this, he wanted me to hand him an empty bottle. So I was taking empty bottles and handing them to him, and he was refilling them with a less expensive wine. We poured the less expensive wine at the table and nobody knew. Customers don't know it, but that kind of shit happens all the time.

Ted LoRusso
Perretti's
New York City

The restaurant where I work now is really great because we only accept reservations for five or more people. And that's it. It's a very trendy place, and all kinds of famous models and actors come in all the time. So people will call up and say, "I'd like to make a reservation for three people tonight at nine," and we'll say, "I'm sorry, we only take reservations for parties of five or more." One night this guy calls up and says that, and I tell him we can't take the reservation, and he says, "Oh I understand that. I don't mean to be a name-dropper, but it's for (famous model)." So I said, "I'm glad you don't mean to be a name-dropper, so why don't you just come in and give your name to the maître d' like everyone else?" and hung up on him.

Another time I was waiting on three supermodels for brunch and they ate like pigs—which is good news for all those women out there who are being brainwashed by the media to be anorexic. You don't have to be—you can be bulimic instead.

I also wait on Robert De Niro a lot and he's great. He just orders what he wants and pays.

Waiter X
Khin Khao
New York City

The most exciting order I ever took was from Robert De Niro. Getting his order was like playing a scene in a movie with him. It was the most focused and concentrated I have ever been. We were discussing Caesar salad and tuna, and it was solemn. Generally I hate waiting on celebrities, and I find that the lesser ones, like television stars, can be a real pain in the ass because they're insecure. But the biggest stars, with few exceptions, are very nice, very sweet, gracious people. It says a lot about the business in general, and how it's all about ego, and how people want to seem important. And the thing about restaurants out here is that most of the people come so that they can see how many people they know. It's like the Maple Drive Strut; if they come in and there's not at least forty people they can wave to they haven't had a good lunch.

> Gregg Ostrin
> Beverly Hills, California

That fucking cow [restaurant critic] Mimi Sheraton used to wear a veil and comb her hair down over her face when she went out to eat. She would do this to be incognito. It's absurd, it's embarrassing. So 325 pounds of hair and mask would come walking into your restaurant and you're not supposed to know who it is. I swear to you. And people respect this woman.

> Gary Chiappa
> Roettele A.G.
> New York City

Mel n' Roses on Melrose Avenue was a happening place a few years back. The biker scene was just taking off. Mickey Rourke and his crew were all over the place, etc. We were packed one Sunday night and I had the front of the restaurant. From the back of the restaurant I saw that a man and a woman had just sat at one of my tables. She was very tall and blond, and rather large like a Swedish massage lady. He was kind of little with dirty hair pulled back in a gross ponytail and had a big biker-dude mustache and dirty clothes. I thought nothing of it; that's what everyone there looked like. I went up and got their drink order and went back to the kitchen. My boss said, "Cara, do you know who that is?" and I said, "No." "That's Michael Jackson." I said, "No way, I saw his face." I took their drinks and went back to the table. Something told me to look at his socks and shoes. When I looked under the table I saw that he had put this entire grungy disguise together but was still wearing sequined socks and penny loafers. At that point I *knew* it was Michael Jackson.

> Cara Green
> Swingers
> Los Angeles, California

Orso is known as a celebrity hangout. People will call and they want to know who's coming in, who's been in, and who's in now. I don't really pay attention to it. One night Al Pacino came in with Robert De Niro. We rarely get people going up to tables for autographs, and if they try to we're supposed to sort of steer them away, or intercept them on the way to the table. So Pacino and De Niro are sitting there and three people came up and asked De Niro for an autograph. Nobody asked Pacino, and he was loving it. I had their table and a few others, including a couple from the suburbs. At this point the manager had pulled me aside and said, "Look, just body block anybody who comes toward their table. Don't let anybody else come to the table." So this table next to them, this suburban couple, were getting pretty drunk and she asked if she could have the menu. I said sure; it's a paper menu, and people like to have them as souvenirs. So she says, "Because I think I want to get an autograph," and I said, *"No! Don't!* Don't even think about it. *I'll lose my job! Please* don't go!" And she said, "Oh, okay, fine, I won't." So after another Sambuca I'm in the front of the restaurant and she goes right to the table. But that happens rarely. A lot of people will look. Even the celebrities will look when somebody like Dustin Hoffman walks into the room. The room will just hush.

Bob Dombroski
Orso
New York City

Children

Life is different today from when I was growing up. By choice or neccessity, many more women are in the workforce now. Women of my mother's generation didn't have the same career oportunities. My mother didn't work outside the house; she stayed home and took care of her children, and each evening prepared a meal for the family. We weren't wealthy, and besides our annual pilgrimage across the country to visit relatives, I don't think we ate out in a restaurant more than once or twice a year. When we did go to a restaurant, strict order was maintained. We were not allowed to get up from the table or raise our voices. This was an era when the reputation of the family was a delicate and important thing, and its preservation was at stake with each public outing.

As I mentioned, things are different in the 1990s. In the first place, many kids don't have a mother and a father anymore; at least not living together in the same house. That just didn't work out. Secondly, people don't eat food that they prepare at home. We have the technology, and a few people still have the know-how, but not one of us has the time. We work eighty hours a week, we go to the gym, we go to the shrink, we go to the twelve-step group of our choice, and we're lucky if we still have the time to go to a restaurant or get take-out before it's time to hit the sack. Thirdly, social order has completely broken down. In this great country we used to care about our reputation in the community; we kept up appearances. Admittedly, it was a stupid motivation, and I was one of the people who rebelled against that sort of thing with a religious fervor, but when I was a kid we didn't bring semiautomatic machine pistols to school, people didn't feel that it was okay to walk around town in a sweatsuit instead of proper clothing, and children behaved in restaurants.

I love children. I love them so much that I'm willing to say that almost everything they do that I don't like is their parents' fault. When I'm in a movie theater watching Madonna take her clothes off in her latest box-office bomb and some three-year-old shouts, "DADDY, WHY IS SHE DOING THAT?" I don't fault the poor child—I wonder why on earth the parent didn't see fit to get a sitter. Likewise when I find myself carrying steaming hot plates of food and dodging toddlers underfoot. Where are the parents, and why have they surrendered the responsibility for their children's safety?

Kitchen doors in restaurants are heavy and they swing open often and with violent force on spring-loaded hinges. Most kitchen doors have a single window at eye level so you can keep from smacking another waiter or customer who is inadvertently standing in front of the door. Unfortunately, you can't see a two-year-old; they're only twenty-four inches tall. You can imagine how bad we all felt when one was knocked across the room in a restaurant where I used to work. Thank God he wasn't seriously injured. If only his parents had been paying attention.

Parents do other cool stuff with their kids. I was waiting on one party who changed their baby right on the table. I didn't mind until the next time I approached the table and the father thrust the feces-laden, wet garment unannounced into my hand; the same hand I would use to pick up your plate, or put bread into a basket for you to eat.

Children are innocent. They mostly do what they're taught or told to do. I wait on some children who are well behaved, but it seems like they are the exception. It's great when it happens. They stay at the table, they throw only a little food, they don't scream too much, and they do something really cute. What's going on out there? Did people forget how to raise kids? How is it that people can afford to eat out but can't afford to get a baby-sitter? And what about the other people who are spending their hard-earned money to have a night out, don't they deserve a little peace? I admit I have a jaundiced view of the picture. I'm a bitter old waiter working in a very adult-oriented restaurant. I'm amazed when someone brings their kids in. I accept the extra work involved: sweeping the floor in an eight-foot radius of the table after the child has left, bringing more bread, more bread, more bread, and trying to decide just which glass to serve milk in, but I don't have the time, energy, or inclination to watch someone else's children while they eat. People have asked me to do this many times, and it's just not my job.

I talked to several waiters and waitresses about waiting on children. Some felt the way I do and some didn't, but what was apparent to me was that the waitpeople from New York City were the most outspoken on this issue. I think that this is because New York City is an adults-only kind of town. Children seem somehow out of place here, so we notice them more. The waiters in other places just accept children as part of their clientele. Bless their hearts.

If children are well behaved it's fine. If they're monsters I don't have a problem with them, I have a problem with the parents. I used to work at this place uptown right near the Beacon Theater. When Sesame Street Live was playing there we were overrun with children. The kids would have just watched Big Bird and whoever on stage for an hour and a half and they would be hyped. They would come into the restaurant and have burgers and several Coca-Colas and they'd be *flying*. The parents would be sick of the whole thing so they would be drinking Bloody Marys, going in the opposite direction. I would be very mean to these children. At that one job in particular I would be very mean. I would trip children. Because they would get upset, and that would send them right back to their parents. I would tell them if they didn't go back to their parents right now that they'd never see them again. I don't have a problem with kids in general, just in restaurants.

Gary Chiappa
Roettele A.G.
New York City

I always cringe when I see them come into my station. I don't mind it if they're well behaved—and I do think their behavior is a *direct* reflection on the parents. I also think it is important for kids to learn to eat out. I remember going out when I was little, and I was well behaved—I had to be. I don't understand why so many kids today are not well behaved. Actually I do understand. What I don't understand is why so many parents let their kids get that way. These kids are demanding, and they don't say please or thank you. That makes me crazy.

Geoff N.
New York City

I'm great at waiting on children, but I would rather hurt them than wait on them. I would rather slap them around outside than have them come into the restaurant. I think the parents who bring their children in are pathetic. You have the choice to have children or not, you chose to have them, now *cook for them*. It depends; some parents have really well-behaved kids. But then you think, those children have been beaten into submission. I've seen all kinds; I've waited on kids who are so spoiled that I was spitting in *their* milkshakes, and I've seen really nice kids who sit quietly through the whole meal. And I'm stuck up; I have almost always worked in places where very few children come.

Ted LoRusso
Perretti's
New York City

I really love children. I'm very tolerant of children because they're children. Many of my friends have kids. It would be nice if people could always get sitters and never took their kids out to restaurants but that's not reality. I have to say that when I'm really busy and a little kid is running around in the restaurant and getting caught in my feet, it's a relief. I like kids. The only kind of kids I don't like are these six-year-olds who come in and are like, "Could I have a café au lait please? And could I have the mocha powder on the side?" It's unnatural.

Waiter X
Khin Khao
New York City

I love kids, so I love to wait on them. There is this great little girl who comes in where I work now. Her name is Tatiana. The first time I saw her she came walking in and started talking my ear off. And she's only three years old. She told Fred, who I work with, "I really want the gnocchi, but I see you don't have it on the menu anymore. I'll have the rigatoni instead." I love her. Every time she comes in we hang out together. I like to give the parents a break, let them eat in peace. I'm probably one of the few waiters who like kids, but I really do.

Stacey Jurewicz
Pescatore
New York City

I like children. I like one child at a time. I like making my fellow waiter wait on the tables while I play with the kid. It seems to me that when parents come in and let me deal with the kid that it's so much easier. It's easier than if they say, "He only eats this, and he only eats that."

Then they're a problem. And after eight o'clock kids should not come in. We're not geared for them. And I don't think the whole society *should* be geared around people who have kids. I mean, I don't work at Chuck E. Cheese. There are places for kids and there are places where kids shouldn't go. Just because we're a restaurant and we're open to the public doesn't mean that it's appropriate to bring kids in here. It's like television—all of television is not "Sesame Street"; the parents have a responsibility to make the appropriate choice. I think that usually when kids are a problem is when their parents have made the wrong choice. Same way when their kids are stealing cars or selling crack.

> Mark Collins
> Universal Grill
> New York City

I don't like waiting on children. Children are not good to bring into a restaurant unless you know that they are going to be good. If it's a little tiny baby I guess it's okay, but then you wonder what it's doing there in the first place. A restaurant seems like a dangerous place to bring a very small child. There are too many things happening too quickly, and too many knives and forks lying around, and too many dishes to break. It's very dangerous. I'm surprised that more people aren't hurt in restaurants.

> Julie Marr
> Orson's
> New York City

How I like waiting on children depends on how well behaved they are. If a kid is running all over a restaurant it annoys the hell out of me. A child can get hurt. They're just an accident waiting to happen. You can trip over them or drop something hot on them if they're allowed to run all over the place. Sometimes I can deal with them okay and sometimes I can't; it depends on my mood. Generally I like children. But some parents will bring infants to a restaurant, and they tend to cry all the way through a meal. That annoys me. As much as a parent wants to go out I think they have a responsibility to the child *and* the other people. It's not fair to the other people in a restaurant if a baby is crying really loud. A parent *can* stay at home and cook. I mean, on the one hand I understand; if I were a parent I would not want to leave my baby at home with someone who is not part of my family. Not in this day and age. But if you want to go out, if you have to go out, leave the infant at home with your *sister*.

Here's another thing: If your child likes to play with things then bring a couple of toys with you. A knife and a fork and a hot candle are not appropriate toys for a young child. Also, when kids play with the cutlery and all the food the cleanup is hell. Some kids make such a big mess. The kids will knock over a glass and break it, or throw tons of food on the floor, and the parents will never even make an attempt to clean up after them.

Michael Marx
Jethro's Bar & Grill
New York City

Babies. The baby phenomenon is one thing I can't stand. E.J.'s was baby heaven. The young mothers are always in a state of emergency, and they think you should be in a state of emergency, too. You know, "Can we get some more crackers *right away*?" because he's going to tear the place up or something. And they come in with all the paraphernalia; the collapsible strollers, everything. It takes them fifteen minutes to get unloaded, they order the food, they eat in five minutes, and then it takes another fifteen minutes to get everything back together. These women won't stay home and make a peanut butter and jelly sandwich for the kid, they've got to go through this thing. And they learn how to be customers real early in that neighborhood, it's scary. All about substitutions and special requests, these scary little monsters who are learning how to be awful customers.

Nancy Kelly
New York City

The best thing about this place is the kids. Because these rich Malibu kids go table hopping just like their parents do, showing off their new cellular phones, talking about deals they're making. I had a sweet sixteen party that I waited on, it was all these sixteen-year-old girls from Bel Air whom you wanted to kill. The girl gets a car phone from her dad and she says, "Daddy, I don't even have a car!" and he goes, "Yes, you do!" and holds out the keys to her new car. We were all joking around saying, "Daddy, I don't have a boyfriend!" "Yes, you do!" and, "But, Daddy, I don't have a job." "Yes, you do, you're now president of Paramount!" You know what I mean? Anything goes out here. I wonder where their values are sometimes.

Robin Shipley
Granita
Malibu, California

Pet Peeves

I am a bitter, hateful waiter. That's not entirely true, but my job really makes me crazy sometimes. I can still put on my game face, smile that I'm-so-glad-to-be-ordered-around-like-a-servant smile, but my heart just isn't in it anymore. And like the Princess and the Pea, little things are starting to get to me. Some of these things are totally irrational, others completely justified, but there are things that the people I wait on do and say that make my pulse higher and my lifespan shorter. They are my pet peeves.

If you have ever waited tables you are going to read what follows and laugh; or grit your teeth and shake your head in a kind of sad recognition. After all, how many times during a shift does a waiter or a waitress corner one of his fellows and regale them with the story of what some jerk at one of his tables just did? If customers could hear what gets said about them in the kitchen I imagine there would be quite a few empty dining rooms. But I suppose talking about the customers behind their backs is probably one of the great joys of every business.

If you have not ever waited tables you might read this and think I'm an asshole. I can live with that.

I'd like to describe some of the things that drive me crazy at work and tell you why they do. I'm doing this for a purely selfish reason—I think it will make me feel better.

One thing I have discovered about my pet peeves is that they come and go, kind of like acne. For instance, it used to really drive me crazy when I would go up to a table and ask if they would like something to drink and I heard the reply, "No, just water." I would have to bite my tongue to keep from asking what they intended to do with the water I was bringing them, other than drink it. Fortunately, this doesn't bother me anymore. To my horror I have even caught myself uttering the dreaded phrase absentmindedly in a restaurant. Go figure.

Some pet peeves are eternal, however; bringing waves of anger to me as faithfully as the tides. One of these is when a customer finishes his food and immediately takes his empty plate and sets it on the table next to his. This drives me insane, and for a number of reasons. First, the assumption is that the waiter is never going to come pick the plate up. In fact, the waiter is never given the chance. Secondly, it's rude. Waiters aren't supposed to clear a table until everyone has finished eating; the reason being that the other diners at the table might feel self-conscious if only their plate remains on the table. And thirdly, your table is your table, that table next to yours is *mine*. I have taken great care to set that table and make it look nice for the people who are going to sit there next. When you set a dirty plate on it chances are I am going to have to strip it and reset it. I don't have time to do that and give you good service, too. Think about it. Finally, like many breaches of etiquette, I wonder if people do this at home. Since most people probably don't have another table at their side in their dining room, do they just drop the plate on the floor? I wonder.

And here's another thing: Why is it that I will set a check down on a table and it will sit there for an hour while the guests gab, but when somebody finally puts some cash or a credit card down they appear as anxious to leave as if the restaurant were on fire? This, after I have walked by the table maybe twenty times in the previous hour. It's a mystery to me. All I can say, and I think this is good advice for anything you might want to do, is plan ahead.

Okay, here's another one: the customer orders coffee and dessert, so I go and get a cup of coffee, a spoon, a creamer, and sugar. I set the sugar and the creamer down in the middle of the table, and the cup of coffee and the spoon to the right hand side of the guest, carefully leaving room in front of the guest for the dessert. I come back to the table with the dessert, and where is the cup of coffee? *Right in front of the guest!* Why? Now I can't serve the dessert.

I can't believe this even happens, so I feel kind of silly discussing it; some people seem to think it's okay to touch waitpeople. It's not. We all hate it. It's like my friend and colleague, Pauline St. Denis, said to me one night, "You don't touch a stripper and you don't touch a waitress." It makes us very angry. Some customers tap at your back while you are trying to take another table's order, and others will actually grab your arm as you are walking by. I always want to ask these people what would happen if I did this to them at their job. What if I came behind your desk and grabbed you? How long do you think it would take for the security guard to arrive?

I am the first to admit that I'm wound a little tight, so I think that I probably have more pet peeves than the average waitperson. The few I mentioned are like a single grain of sand on a long stretch of beach. After all, I don't want to appear too mean spirited. (How about when a young female customer won't even look at you, ordering everything through her date? I mean, what year is it anyway?) And in fairness to the restaurant customers of the world, I realize we're all human, and we all have different standards of appropriate behavior. And anyway, it's the waiter's job to suck it up and smile, smile, smile. But I was curious about what sends other waiters around the bend, so I asked them if they had any pet peeves. They did.

The thing that's the worst is when they go, "I'd like a cup of coffee," and you go and get the coffee and they say, "I'd like a glass of water," and you come back with the water and they ask, "Do you have any sugar?" so you come back with the sugar and they say, "Oh, I'd like a gin and tonic," and then you ask, "Does anyone want anything else while I'm here?" and they all say, "No, no, no," and you come back with the gin and tonic and they say, "Ooh, that looks good. I'll have one of those." When people do that now I say, "You're a radio, I'm switching you off," and I walk away from the table. And they love it, because I work in a trendy restaurant and we're allowed to be nasty. People think it's charming.

I also hate it when people touch me. I hate it because it demonstrates the underlying belief system that people have about waiters, which is that we are machines without spirits or feelings. I mean, I don't go grabbing my customers or pawing their jewelry with my greasy fingers. It makes me really upset.

Waiter X
Khin Khao
New York City

I would say that I genuinely like about 20 percent of my customers, and there are another 30 percent that I can force myself to like on a good day. The other 50 percent drive me right up a wall. They are just complete idiots with no social skills whatsoever. I have a list of pet peeves: 1) Sitting at a dirty table when every table around them is clean. 2) Turning around and staring at you because they "desperately" need something. 3) When they *demand* things—never mind saying please or thank you. 4) When they ask for something different every time I go to the table. 5) When they sit at a table for hours and don't take that into consideration when they leave a tip. 6) Getting up and going to the waitstation instead of asking you for something. 7) Asking the waitstaff to change things about the restaurant (music, fans, windows, lighting) that should have gone into the restaurant selection process. 8) Europeans. I could go on and on, but I'll stop here.

Amy Packard
New York City

People who have special diets should just stay home and eat. I want to say, "Why don't you stay at home?" They go through the whole thing, no butter, no Parmesan, no onions ("I'm allergic. I'm allergic to onions"). I don't think anybody is allergic to onions, but they say they're allergic to them. Or they'll say they are allergic to butter, but they'll have cream in their coffee so it doesn't make sense. Those kind of people drive me nuts. I also dislike people who ignore me. I'll come to the table and say, "Would you like something to drink?" and they just keep talking. I just leave and wait until they call me over. There was a group of eight people, four couples from Long Island; big hair, and big makeup. One had a gold lamé bib that she put on over her sparkly blazer. They were going to a matinee. They were in their sixties, and the women were all done up gaudy. They called me over and said they should order because they had to get to the theater. I got two orders and the other couples started talking about these colored eye pencils. One woman said, "I like the hardness and the softness of them," and another woman said, "I like the Lancôme because of the softness of them." They were going on about the hardness and the softness of these colored pencils, and I'm just standing there. I mean, they had called me over to take the order. I said, "Excuse me, I would love to hear about these pencils but I should get your order because you're going to the theater." And one woman said, "He doesn't want to hear about the pencils," and another woman says, "No, he *does* want to hear about the pencils!" They went back and forth like that for about three more minutes and I finally just walked away.

Bob Dombrowski
Orso
New York City

There's one thing that really drives me insane, especially in New York. And it comes back to the fact that the human being is the last link in the food chain. Most people grow up in a very citified environment and they have no idea what it's like to have to go out and catch your own food. And in order to survive we're getting further and further away from that. As a result I think people are becoming very unrealistic about what it is that they eat and how they sustain themselves. At our restaurant we have a couple of classic dishes on the menu, and one of them is a coho salmon. It's a whole small salmon—head off, filleted, and stuffed with crabmeat. The problem is that it still has the skin on it. Often I've taken it out to a table and put it down in front of someone and they say, "Oh, I can't possibly eat this." And there is nothing wrong with it except that the skin is on. I guess these people never went fishing when they were kids. And the thing about being in New York City is that there are thousands and thousands of people who are going starving every day, and these people don't give it a second thought. That's really my biggest peeve. I mean we all have lots of little things that drive us crazy, but that someone would send food back because they have a psychological barrier to seeing skin on a fish is too much. I had a woman send back a piece of salmon last night because it had bones in it. It was a salmon steak, center-cut, so the backbone goes right through it. She couldn't bear to touch the bones. We had to pick it up, take it back to the kitchen, and throw it in the garbage. You can't use it, or serve it again. It's disgusting. You see the poverty on the streets around you all the time and people don't even give it a second thought.

Chico Garcia
Midnight Lake
New York City

There's a list of maybe five hundred things that piss me off, like when they breathe I get pissed off. At the top of the list is men who automatically call me honey, or baby, or sweetheart, and I got a lot of that at the last restaurant where I worked because of that culture, you know, the way they treat women is like shit. They just felt it was their divine right since I was waiting on their table. In fact, the night before I got laid off this really disgusting old man with gnarly teeth and stuff was looking over the dessert menu and he says, "How about I have you for dessert?" If only I had known I was about to be laid off I could have said what I really wanted to say. That's probably the top of the list, that type of behavior. Or when somebody would physically touch me, because that's such an invasion. And people do that a lot, like to get your attention they'll pull you over to a table. And for some reason, more so than if someone bumps into me on the street, that bothers me. I also used to get sick of people who would ask for things in a real demanding way and would never say please or thank you. I think it's because I try to be courteous when I go into a restaurant, or anywhere. I try to treat people with respect, it's just basic courtesy. My six-year-old, he doesn't get anything without please or thank you. And a real frustration comes up because you can't do anything about it; if other people do that to you out in the civilian world you can call them on it. You can say, "Excuse me, what's your problem?" or "You're a rude son of a bitch." That's one of the most frustrating things about waiting tables; you're put out there as a slave-for-hire and your hands are tied behind your back. Unless you have a great manager who will back you up, you have to deal with whatever people dish out. People come in with their own little agendas and their own little trips. You have to do it to understand it—if you try to tell somebody who's never waited tables they wouldn't believe it. People come in and they *like* ordering you around. They *like* to send their food back. It's like they never got their needs met when they were four years old so they're going to make you be their mother now. "I don't like this, take it off the bill." That's another thing; people come in and want to get something and then not pay for it.

Bridget Munger
Arthur's Landing
Weehawken, New Jersey

One of the things I don't like—I'll start with dessert and coffee—is when I bring them two cups of coffee and one has regular and one has decaf and they say, "Is that the decaf?" *Like I'm stupid.*

Last week some guy walked in and sat at a table for four. He was a party of two, and he took the napkin from the other place setting before I could get it off the table and picked up his silverware and put the napkin down and then put his silverware down on top of it. So I said I need to clear some of these things off the table, and he said, "I don't want my silverware touching the table." The silverware had been sitting on the tablecloth when he came in, so they had *already* touched the table. He was living in a total fucking dreamworld.

I hate it when people want to sit at a table for four when they are two people. I work in an eight-table restaurant, and they just don't understand.

I hate it when people ask for dressing on the side, just a few slices of lemon, or when they ask what kinds of dressings you have when you only have one and it's written on the menu.

Cyndi Raftus
Hourglass Tavern
New York City

Waiting tables pays the bills, and it can be fun when the customers are pleasant. When they're not it is hell. I hate customers who have too many requests, like, "I want the linguini with clams, but can you make that with angel hair, put shrimp instead of clams, pesto sauce instead of tomato, extra garlic, and just a touch of basil?" I mean, what the hell? Or they ask you to put the dressing or sauce on the side and the first thing they do is pour it all on the food.

Dimitri Rathschech
New York City

Here's one: "I'm catching a plane. I'm in a hurry because I'm catching a plane." Don't lie to me. *I know you're lying*. Saturday night in Santa Monica; I'm upstairs and we're packed—totally packed. It's 8:55 and this guy says, "I have to catch a plane at 9:10." I wanted to smack him. I said, "Why didn't you tell me when you walked in?" The guy ordered trout. It takes a long time. If he had told me he was in a hurry I would have definitely suggested he *not* order trout. I said, "You're telling me now you have to leave in ten minutes? I'm sorry." So I bring the food to the table and they ask for a check. I said, "Do you want me to wrap this up for you?" and they said no. So I said, "Eat plane food then."

Another pet peeve is when they order coffee and you bring it to the table with sugar and half-and-half. Then they say, "Is that half-and-half or milk?" and I say, "Did you ask for milk? Because I didn't hear you ask for milk so I brought what we always serve, which is half-and-half." If you tell them it's milk, they want half-and-half; if you tell them it's half-and-half, they want milk. Then you bring it and they go, "Do you have Sweet 'n Low?" They'll run you to death if you don't tell them off. They'll say, "I'd like a cup of coffee," and you have to say, "LISTEN! IF YOU WANT COFFEE, IF YOU WANT MILK, IF YOU WANT HALF-AND-HALF, IF YOU WANT SUGAR, OR IF YOU WANT

SWEET 'N LOW, TELL ME RIGHT NOW! *BECAUSE I AIN'T GOING BACK!"* Then they learn to order.

Becky Milici
Fama
Santa Monica, California

My biggest pet peeve lately, since I seem to be getting this one a lot lately, is when people flag you down and say, *"Excuse me,* we're ready to order," and you walk up to the table and they look at each other and say, "What are you going to have?" and then it's, "You go first." "No, you go first." And I have to say, "Excuse me, you said you were ready—I took you at your word. When you *are* ready, feel free to call me over, but until then I will be at another table." I'll tell you my waiter theory, which I think should be passed into law by Congress: you should not be allowed into a restaurant until you have worked in one. It should be like a country club where you have a pass. At the door you would have to say, "Yes, that's right, I worked at Denny's." Because the best people to wait on are other waiters; they know how screwed up it is.

Shit, I've got a lot of pet peeves. Oh, here's one, "What kind of salad dressing do you have?" and I say, "Bleu Cheese, Thousand Island, and Vinaigrette." Then the customer asks, "Do you have any Ranch?" I say, "Let me repeat myself, Bleu Cheese, Thousand Island, and Vinaigrette. Either I'm lying to you or I just decided to delete this option for you." There is a whole psychology behind it. People sometimes treat you as if you're witholding information from them. You are the enemy. You're not giving them what they want. They don't trust you. Oh, okay, pet peeve: this one I get a lot, too, "Is your Caesar salad very good?" "Yes, it's very good." *"Oh,* like you'd tell me anything else!" *"Well, why the hell did you ask me?* What am I, a liar? *I don't give a damn if you get the Caesar salad or the damn Cobb salad!"* It's true, though, it's like they almost want to trust you but you've got something up your sleeve and they know it.

Doug V.
Los Angeles, California

I have several pet peeves concerning customers. I hate it when you can see everything in their mouths while they eat, and there are some people with really big mouths who do that especially well. And then there's, "Do you have a cigarette?" and I'll say, "No, I don't smoke," and they'll say, "Well, does somebody else? Can you get me one?" But the big one would have to be The Tap. You know, when you're at another table and they're tapping you on the back to get your attention. Oh, man. I mean, would they want another table to do that when I'm talking to them?

Eileen Schwartz
West Lynn Cafe
Austin, Texas

I don't like it when they ask me my name and try to pretend that they're being friendly with me. What they really want is to be able to get my attention more effectively. All night they'll be saying, "Shawna, Shawna!"

But this is the worst: they say, "What kind of beers do you have?" and you say, "Rolling Rock, Bud, Corona, Pearl, and Modello." And they go, "Do you have Beck's?" And you say, "I just told you what we have." And they'll ask for another one, "St. Pauli Girl?" and you have to say, "We only have the beers I told you we have. We don't have any other brands."

Shawna Mason
Lone Star Roadhouse
New York City

You've probably heard them all before. "Would you like anything to drink?" "No, I'll have a glass of water." Just the real simple things. They ask you a question and they don't wait to hear you answer it. I don't really have any real concrete pet peeves.

Garrett Harker
San Francisco, California

I hate it when customers give you "tips," meaning advice. If the tip is not in cash I don't want it. I think I'm pretty easygoing, but I despise a customer touching me. Because I just wouldn't walk up and touch another person.

Gary Chiappa
Roettele A.G.
New York City

I hate when I come up to a table and I'm standing there and people just continue to talk. I'm *signing,* trying to get them to acknowledge me. I work with some people who have no shame about going, "EXCUSE ME FOR IN-TERRUPTING!" but I can't do that. I also hate it when people won't look at me when they order. Here's another one: you ask a woman what she would like to drink and she whispers to the guy, *"I'll have a white wine spritzer."* Then he looks at you and says, "She'll have a white wine spritzer." I guess it's kind of cute in an out-dated sort of way, but I just hate it. Another thing I hate is when a customer asks me my name and then proceeds to *use* it. Something you'll find working in Beverly Hills is that customers will come in and order a dish and then proceed to reconstruct it. No salt, no sauce, no butter, no oil, do you have this instead of that, and so on. I'm thinking, why don't you just eat at home? Buy a piece of salmon, grill it up, steam some vegetables; it will cost you ten bucks. What are you paying $30 for? To give me a hard time? I don't need this, go home! I don't get it.

Gregg Ostrin
Beverly Hills, California

I hate it when customers don't listen to you. Like when you go up to a table and they're having a conversa-tion and you wait until there's a break and then you say,

"Excuse me," and they don't acknowledge you. And you wait, and you wait, and they *still* don't acknowledge you. That drives me up the wall. It's like, I'm there to take the order if they can *please* just talk to me. Because if you walk away they start bitching, "Where's the waitress?" It's a no-win situation. It also drives me crazy when people will calculate the tip on their credit cards to make the total an even number. I hate that, because it's going to come out an odd number on the bill anyway because of the interest. It's also hard when people ask you what is good. Because people have different tastes. I never know what to say, except that I like this or that. If they say what is *your* favorite thing on the menu it's much easier.

Jackie Becke
Los Angeles, California

I hate it when I'm at a table and I'm saying something and I have to repeat it to every single customer. Another thing that has happened a lot lately is that I'll go to a table with three guys and three women and I'll take the women's orders. Then I go to the first guy and he'll motion to the women like I should take their orders first. He isn't even paying attention to the fact that I've done it already. Or people who insist that they deserve something different from what they're getting. We don't do substitutions where I work, you get what you get. And people get adamant about it; they're mean if they don't get it, they cause a stink—as if they're a special person.

Ray Proscia
Georgia
West Hollywood, California

My most recent pet peeve is when you take the check and the money away, and they don't want change, and then a few minutes later they tell you they want the receipt. THE RECEIPT IS ON THE BOTTOM OF THE CHECK! They can just take it off themselves, but for some reason they just won't do it.

Another one is when you have some macho guy at the head of the table and he calls you over because he wants to order. Of course, there are three other people at the table, and none of them is ready. So you have to stand there for ten minutes. I have better things to do with my time; my other tables need things, too.

I also hate it when people won't let you take their glasses away. I've had a woman actually slap my hand because I tried to take a glass with $1/8$ of an inch of back-wash in it. It's like, are you really going to drink that?

I also dislike it when people order things on the side. If you're that picky, eat at home. I mean, they'll tell you they are on a diet, and then they will invariably order dessert. It makes no sense.

Stacey Jurewicz
Pescatore
New York City

I hate it when—and I know this isn't really their fault— but I hate it when I'm really, really busy, and I have fifty things in my head, and I'm going down the line, you know how you sort of have it organized, the things you have to do and the order you have to do them in, and you're like, after I do the next five things I'm going to bring bread to that table. But that table flags you down and says, "Can we have some bread now, *please*?" It's like, "I know that you need bread. I'm not stupid." I've actually said that.

Also, people who won't leave at the end of the night. They've had coffee, they've had dessert, you've turned all the machines off, everything is put away, all the chairs are on the tables, and they're still fucking sitting there. And then, inevitably the guy turns to you and says, "Are we keeping you?" and I'm like, "Do you need a brick house to fall on you?"

Oh, I actually had a guy whistle for my attention once. This was at a gross restaurant in Boston. I turned around and lost it on him, my head was going back and forth—I looked like Linda Blair. I said, "If you want my attention you say excuse me, and treat me with respect and dignity."

Rebecca Hall
Hourglass Tavern
New York City

I try not to let anything affect me too much. I try to laugh it off, but I get a little aggravated when I'll ask, "Would anyone like anything?" and one person will ask for a beer, and I ask, "Would anyone else like a beer?" and nobody says anything, and I go to the bar, which in my restaurant is a long way, and come back with the beer, and then somebody will say, "You know what? I'll have one of those, too."

I had a woman ask for a half decaf, half regular the other night. I don't do that. And another thing that bothers me is this: we don't carry decaf espresso, and the other night a woman says, "I'd like a decaf cappuccino." And I said, "We don't have decaf espresso." And she said, "Well, I want a decaf cappuccino." And I told her, "You need decaf espresso to make a decaf cappuccino." And she says, "Okay, I'll just have a regular cappuccino then." Instead of having a brewed decaf, she wants a regular cappuccino. Do they know what they want?

When I worked at Benny's Burritos people would come in and go, "I'll have a margarita." And you would have to say, "Okay, Sauza? Three Generations? Cuervo? Up? On the Rocks? Frozen? Salt? No Salt? Come on, help me out here!" We used to go crazy. People say they want a margarita and there's eighty different ways to have a margarita. And when I was at Gotham it was the same thing with martini's. People would say, "I'll have a martini." And it's like, "Okay, gin? Vodka? Up? On the rocks? Twist? Olives? Come on, man!" Same thing with beer, "I'll have a beer." Do they want me to choose for them? You kind of have to hold people's hands, they're like babies.

Russell Dean Anderson
Miracle Grill
New York City

The one thing I cannot stand is when you are in the middle of one thing and they ask you for another. You're clearing away the dishes and they say, "I'd like a cup of coffee." It makes me want to drop the dishes on the floor and run and get them the cup of coffee. It's like, what the fuck do you want me to do? And I tell them, "Just let me take care of this, and then I'll get you a cup of coffee." But you have to do it in a nice manner. I suppose if I was working in New York I could really tell them how I feel, but not out here. That's my biggest pet peeve. I've changed as a waiter. It used to be if I was having a bad day, everyone was going to have a bad day. My service reflected my mood. Now I become Waitron—I go on autopilot and just do what has to be done. It's maturity. When I was younger I didn't give a shit. I needed the job, but I knew if I got fired I could just hit the road and do something else. There was a romanticism to it. Now I have to be more pragmatic. I can't wear my emotions on my sleeve.

Dan Shapero
San Francisco, California

Try waiting tables at a Beverly Hills "industry" restaurant. You'll find that the way your customers breathe becomes a pet peeve.

Sam K.
Rox
Beverly Hills, California

I hate it when people put their dirty plates on the table next to them. I even hate it when they stack their plates up on their own table. And when I go out to eat I sometimes want to do it. But I still hate it when they do it to me. Then I think that it shouldn't bother me. But it does because it makes me feel like I'm not doing my job. And that's usually not the case.

Kelsey Geisler
Trompe L'oeil
New York City

Everything that drives me crazy can be fine if it's done with a proper amount of respect. Like when someone asks your name. There are these big corpulent guys who come in and smoke cigars and say, "What's your name, honey?" and then there are nice people who honestly want to know your name to establish some sort of relationship.

I hate it when somebody asks me what they should order and I don't know them. Because you know that whatever you recommend they're going to hate it, and then you'll lose money. And if you don't suggest anything they think you're being snotty.

> Jennifer
> L'acajou
> New York City

A really gross thing is finding meat under the table. And this has happened more often than one would think, when you're the closing waiter and you're cleaning up at the end of the night. I'm not talking about people dropping stuff, I'm talking about when they have a piece of gross gristle or something and they throw it on the floor because they don't want to put it back on their plate. I mean, would you do that at home?

> Lars Goransson
> Austin, Texas

One thing I really hate is when they say *get me.* They say, "Get me this, or get me that," when they ask for something. They're ordering you around. It's just not to their advantage to do that.

> Freeda Kaufman
> Jethro's Bar & Grill
> New York City

I hate it when customers sit down without letting you greet them and then get an attitude when they realize they don't have menus. It also bugs me when they order at the door.

Malika Simmons
Around the Clock
New York City

I think my biggest pet peeve is when people don't use basic, rudimentary table manners. Well, you can sit with your elbows on the table now and that's kind of okay, but when the waiter comes you're supposed to sit up straight. This guy the other night was sitting with his elbows on the table and I had to clear away his plate, and it was like he played football in high school, you know? He was trying to hide it, and then as I reached around to get the plate he looked down at it like, gee, I wonder how this fucker's going to get this plate out of here with me covering it so well? The coach would be proud.

Another thing is not putting that napkin in their lap so I can't serve them. But I believe in shame as a motivating factor. I just say, "Would you like me to put that napkin in your lap or would you rather I put this scalding hot plate of food in your lap. You pick." People appreciate that. They like to be told what to do. My friend Kim once told me that people will pay more for dominance. Whether it's on a phone line, from a hooker, or from a waiter. When you dominate them like that it works.

Also, I hate it when people ask me what they should eat. They'll say, "What do you suggest?" and then don't believe me when I tell them. Everybody knows what they want to eat, I don't care what anybody says. It's like playing Jeopardy, you go with your impulse, you know? They look at the menu and I'll say, "What sounds good to you?" and they'll say, "This sounds good, and this sounds good, and this sounds good." And usually the first thing they say is what they really want and what they want you to reinforce them for. But invariably some schmuck sitting at the same table goes, "Oh, he's going to say everything's good." It's so stupid. Why would I tell you something's really good when it's shit and in fifteen minutes you're going to find out? I'm going to deny the murder when I know that proof positive that I commited it will be presented in minutes? And I have to remind them of that every time. I have to say, "You know, I'm not going to lie to you because, first of all, my salary, which you are paying, hangs in the balance, and secondly, you will find me out. You're going to get a plate of food that tastes like shit, and I'm going to say it's the best stuff in the world, and then what's going to happen? One of us is going to look like a fucking idiot."

Mark Collins
Universal Grill
New York City

I doubt if I'll say anything too original, but the old one where the customer asks two waiters for the same thing and they both bring it still gets to me. I remember this waiter bitched me out about it one time and I never forgot it. Another thing would probably be when people ask me stupid questions, like, "Do you know where the bathroom is?" I mean, of course I know where the bathroom is, I work here. It's such a dumb question. Oh, and when people call you over from across the restaurant to take their order and it turns out that they're not ready. That's a pet peeve because it interferes with your work. But basically I want to treat people in a restaurant the way I like to be treated, so I try to be courteous, and kind, and be attentive without going over the top. That's how I work.

Michael K.
The Grill
Beverly Hills, California

I hate it when people insist on putting their legs out in the aisle. After one or two times of saying excuse me I just won't say it anymore. And if I happen to kick them I am not going to say I'm sorry. I never do that. They're ignoring me by putting their feet out in the aisle so I'm going to ignore them and not care. I'll step on their foot, right on it, and just keep walking.

Then there are people who come in and say, "I want the sole with no sauce. I'd like it broiled and dry." She wants it broiled dry? So she pays $25 for a dry slab of sole. If you don't want to eat that way don't go out to the restaurant. That's my pet peeve, people who want to come in and rewrite the menu.

Another thing is, there will be a party of ten people and they show up one at a time. And then the second they sit down they expect to have a drink. They expect you to run over to them and get them a drink that second. And you know, I have a lot of other tables.

It also really gets to me when people start the evening with complaint. For those people my tactic is to ignore them until they're waving at me to come over. I'll just ignore them. If they're going to come in and try to dictate how warm or cool the room should be, how loud the music should be, how bright or dark the room should be, then they should stay home. Why should one person dictate how it's going to be for everyone else in the restaurant?

> Michael Marx
> Jethro's Bar & Grill
> New York City

I can't stand when people say, "Can you check and see if our order is ready?" I want to say to them, "What do you think I do all night long? You see me go in and out of that swinging door a hundred times a minute; what do you think I do in there? I don't have to check, I've *been* checking on your order." That I can't stand.

I also hate when people claim that they have an allergy to something just because they want you to take it back and bring them something they like.

> Nancy Kelly
> New York City

Don't touch me. Tip me, always, because I deserve it. Don't ask me my name, because I'm going to tell you it's, uh, George. Or, Waiter. I don't want my name screamed out across a restaurant. I don't want to be your friend, you don't want me to be your friend. I'm here to bring you food, give it to you with a big smile, and that's about it. Also, I'm polite, and I like polite back. I don't like to be bossed. And don't snap your fingers at me. I'm not a taxi-cab or a dog.

Another thing I don't like is when people take things from other tables. And when they put their coats on the chairs at another table. I become a bitch; I walk over and say, "We have a place for those coats," and they say, "We'll move them when someone comes." And I tell them, "It's going to be hard to seat that table with your stuff all over it."

A major pet peeve is when people want things changed. People who come to a restaurant and say, "I want the salmon you have, but can you do it without the sauce, and with a piece of bread?" It's the *Five Easy Pieces* syndrome. That's a scene I hate more than any-thing, because I'm *not* on his side. I want to tell him to go back in the kitchen and put a hocker on that bread and spread it around. The only thing I don't like about him is that he lost it.

Ted LoRusso
Perretti's
New York City

Tipping

Okay, let's talk about tipping. I live and work in New York City so I consider myself fortunate; most people who eat out here know how to tip and they do the right thing. I only receive a bad tip a few times a night. When I first started waiting tables in Oklahoma it was not at all unusual to get stiffed or receive a very poor tip (10 percent or less). Don't get me wrong, I have nothing against Okies; after all, I am one. I'm just stating a fact.

I believe people tip poorly for several reasons: they don't understand the tipping system or know the appropriate amount to leave; they're cheap; they feel they have genuinely received poor service; or they are mean and spiteful. Of course, some people may leave a bad tip for more than one reason; they could conceivably be mean, spiteful, and cheap, for instance.

Nobody really knows how the tipping system originated. I once heard that it started in England when some business-man figured out that if he slipped his waitperson a little coin he got served faster, and therefore could get back to work sooner, which I guess is desirable to some people. I find this story unbelievable, since our friends from across the pond are notoriously bad tippers. My first boss (who was a real restaurant warhorse) told me that the word *tips* is actually an acronym for To Insure Proper Service. Sounds good to me. However it got started, the tipping system seems to be here to stay.

In the United States the proper amount to tip a waiter is 15 to 20 percent of the total of the check. As Bryan Miller writes in *The New York Times*, "In effect, that money is not really a gratuity—that is, a thank you for service performed—but the waiter's salary. Restaurateurs interviewed said that if the tip system did not exist, the food prices would be 15 to 20 percent higher. Therefore, they said, it is not fair to use a tip as a weapon, something to be handed out in direct proportion to a waiter's performance."[1]

I should take a moment to explain how most waiters and waitresses are compensated. According to federal minimum wage laws, tipped employees must be payed at least $2.65 an hour by their employers. So we are all payed $2.65 an hour. Of course, we are also taxed on this amount. Additionally, we have taxes withheld from our paychecks on an amount of money that equals about 8 percent of the total of all the dinner checks we write. The government requires this so that waiters pay taxes on their tips, which the IRS assumes will be at least 8 percent. The net effect of this is that after taxes and social security have been witheld, we usually receive no money at all in our paychecks, and sometimes they indicate a negative amount. Also, because the government assumes that you will receive at least an 8 percent tip, and in fact taxes you as if you did, a table that stiffs you (leaves no tip at all) has actually taken money from your pocket. Nice. The upshot of all this is that whatever is in your pocket when you walk out the restaurant door is what you have to live on.

As a waiter you must accept the fact that you work for tips.

[1] Bryan Miller, "Restaurant Tipping: Many Fingers Make Light Pockets," *The New York Times*, 12 July 1992

This has several practical implications. One is that you are completely at the mercy of your customers for your income. Any customer can get up and walk out the door without leaving you a cent after he has sat in your station for an hour and a half and taken up a considerable amount of your time and energy. Another is that your income can fluctuate wildly depending on the amount of business the restaurant is doing. I have left work at the end of the night without cab fare to get home and I have left with my rent money (I have a very cheap rent). And it is a given that if you really need money it will be a slow night.

I believe the tipping system is good for the customers. Most waiters work very hard at their jobs and genuinely try to give the best service possible. After all, the customer is directly paying their salary. And most customers honor the system and leave a fair amount of money. I admit it must seem unfair to some people to have to leave additional money on top of the bill, but look at it this way: when you go to any other service-oriented establishment, say a doctor's office or a law firm, you give them a significantly larger amount of money and leave with an empty stomach.

Restaurant owners think the tipping system is great, because they don't have to pay their waitstaff. Ultimately, I think it works to their disadvantage. Most waiters have absolutely no loyalty to the restaurant where they work or to the people who own it. When the business falls off, we start looking for the next job. Also, the management style of most restaurant owners and managers doesn't really foster much loyalty, so why not go where the money, at least, is good?

I think the most significant effects of the tipping system are the psychological ones. As a waiter working for tips, on a certain level you feel like a beggar or a servant; scrounging for whatever your benefactors see fit to give you. This is not a good feeling. And your customers do little to dispel this notion, saying clever things like, "Your tip depends on it!" or the ever-popular, "There goes your tip!" In the end, the tipping system is as psychologically empowering to customers as it is debilitating to the waiters. But we all know the score when we tie on an apron.

I have been the recipient of more than one great tip. When I was sixteen a woman left me $200 on a $34 check. Women have also left me their telephone numbers, which is a nice personal touch. And every waiter will tell you that it's always a pleasure to wait on other waiters—they're friendly, they're no trouble at all, and they always leave at least 20 percent.

On the down side, it is pointless to talk about people who don't tip at all, because that is simply inexcusable. But I would like to mention a situation where a 15 percent tip is just not satisfactory. I recently waited on a bachelorette party. The reservation was for ten people at 7:30 on a Friday night. At about 8:00 they started to come straggling in, and by 9:30 there were only eight people at the table. Now this gets under my skin for a few reasons. First, tardiness is bad form; it's very rude to your dinner companions. Secondly, when a party (and especially a large party) is late it can disrupt the flow of traffic in a restaurant for an entire evening. Most restaurants depend on using a table more than once a night, because they couldn't keep their doors open on the income from one seating. If you have ever gone to a restaurant and wondered why your table, the one you reserved, isn't ready, it's probably because the party before you showed up late. Anyway, these women were all late. As they waited for their friends to show up they drank several cocktails and a few glasses of wine each. At 9:30 I convinced them to order. By the time they finished eating it was almost 11:00, and they were all in various stages of drunkenness. I was about to ask if they would like dessert and coffee when one of them turned a little green and headed for the bathroom. In the restaurant where I work our bread station is in the hallway that leads to the bathrooms. The bread station consists of a large metal shelving unit that has a two-drawer bread warmer on the bottom shelf, a heavy wooden cutting board on the middle shelf, and bags of fresh bread on the top shelf. Suffice to say, she didn't make it to the bathroom and instead chose to throw up on the cutting board. Not the floor; on the *cutting board*. Of course, the waitstaff has to clean up this kind of mess, and it's not very pleasant. The point being that when I gave them their check at midnight I had been waiting on them for four hours and cleaning up their vomit. For this I received a 15 percent tip. It is my feeling that I gave them quite a bit of extra service, not to mention that I was deprived of the income I would have made from the party that was supposed to sit at the same table at 9:30.

I have a lot of stories like that one, as every waiter does. In the end you always feel unappreciated and terribly self-righteous. As a rule, I never look at my tips (the exception being larger parties, when it is always advisable to count the money and make sure there is enough to at least cover the check). I started this practice about four years ago and it has served me well. I finally figured out that no matter how much I worried about my individual tips, I was going to leave at the end of the night with the same amount of money. So why bother? My new approach is to try and give everyone good service and hope for the best. This is made possible by the way we handle money in our restaurant. Generally, we take the money to the host, who rings it in to the cash register and puts our tips into our tip cup. At the end of the night we count our tips, give the bartender 10 percent (the standard tip-out for bartenders in New York City) and pocket the rest.

I asked the waiters and waitresses I met if they had any interesting tip stories, and how they feel about working for tips. As I expected, everyone had pretty strong feelings about this issue.

I think the tipping system is a fair system. But people do abuse it like crazy. I hate to say it, but Europeans don't tip. I had always heard of people going after tables to ask if there was something wrong with the service, just to find out why they got a bad tip. I had never done anything like that. If I got a shitty tip I got a shitty tip, that's the way it goes. But at the restaurant I work at now we get a lot of Europeans, and they either think the service is included or pretend to think it's included, and it's disgusting. You should know the tipping customs wherever you go. Or at least ask. I really appreciate it when someone says, "Is it included or not?" And I make sure they know that I appreciate it.

Anyway, until this job I had never mentioned a bad tip to a customer, but I've now had to do it a couple of times. There was a situation where I busted my tail for three hours and there was exact change on the table. I went up to them as they were about to leave and said, "Is there a problem? There is no tip here." I said, "I hate doing this, but I just want to know if there was a problem with my service." And of course they acted all innocent, "Oh, there wasn't anything there? We left $20 on that table." They were insistent that they had left me $20. So I said, "Oh, you left me $20? Fine then, don't worry about it." And they said, "No, no, no, here," and then it gets really weird and uncomfortable.

I had another table recently that were Scandinavians, who must have had forty beers on their check. And ironically, I'm half Swedish. That's all they did, drink round after round of beers. They were really obnoxious and rude, and they were smoking a ton, and the check was $135. They left me $4. I had made maybe thirty trips to this table, and in our restaurant that's a big deal because we are so busy. I grabbed one of the guys and said, "You know what? I don't know if you guys know this, but this is not a big enough tip." And he said, "No, we're waiters." And I said, "Well then, what's up?" The guy said he thought I did a lousy job because I didn't clear all the empty bottles or empty the ashtrays fast enough. It blew me away. If they were waiters they should know that at their rate of consumption you can't keep up with that.

Tom Andonian
Los Angeles, California

I hate working for tips; it's degrading. But I get even. If a customer doesn't leave me 20 percent I hunt them down and shoot them.

Alexandra Lee
New York City

The worst is when people joke about tips. They'll say, "It'll come off your tip!" Just don't bring it up, it's humiliating anyway. And I usually say. "That's okay, I don't work for tips, I'm doing this for research." Just to use it, to talk about it, bugs me. And I've been out with friends who do that and it mortifies me. I'll go and find the waiter and apologize. It's the worst.

> Bob Dombroski
> Orso
> New York City

Recently I have left the restaurant with *no* money, and naturally, it sucks. The money situation angers me. I don't mind working for tips when I get them, but I don't like going to work and sitting on my ass when it's slow.

> Sebastian Elliot
> The Riviera
> New York City

When you pool tips you don't even think about it. On the other hand I'm so codependent that if I don't change the customer's life I'm not doing my job. I feel like I have to bond with them, move them, it gets bad. I'm in therapy, okay? So I don't even look at my tips, to tell you the truth.

> Robin Shipley
> Granita
> Malibu, California

Generally, I like working for tips. However, it does open you up to all kinds of abuse from the customers. Some days I feel like saying, "Hi, I'll be your waitress today. You are paying my rent, how may I be your slave?" Most people don't realize that when they don't tip we have to pay income tax on 8 percent of their check anyway.

> Robin Maynor
> Linn's Fruit Bin
> Cambria, California

I can tell if somebody is not going to tip me. And if they are not going to tip me I will add the service charge. I don't care if it's one person or six people, I'll just add it on. If I don't add it on and I get a bad tip I always say something. I used to be too shy to say anything but then I realized that this is my work; I'm making the effort to serve these people, if they have a problem they should talk to me about it. I think it's hard to work for tips. You have to separate yourself from it.

Shawna Mason
Lone Star Roadhouse
New York City

I had one guy refuse to leave me a tip because I wouldn't call him a cab. Have you ever tried to call a cab in New York? Car service? I don't understand, what do you want? I said, "You walk out in the street and stick your arm out, that's about how it goes." And he was like, totally foreign, but I was over it. And he was really mad at me, that I wouldn't do it. And I thought I was sort of nice about explaining how it works. He just refused to leave me any money.

Rebecca Hall
Hourglass Tavern
New York City

In New York people tipped much better than they do out here. Much better. I don't have a problem working for tips, as long as customers understand that's what's going on. It really bothers me when I wait on a table and really go out of my way to give them amazing service and they leave a 10 percent tip. Because I'm a really good waiter. And with people like that you could throw up on their table and they would leave the same money. That bothers me. If you don't have it that's one thing, but it's as if they don't recognize the difference between good service and bad service.

I have a good tip story. Julia Roberts and Charlie Sheen came with Oliver Stone into the restaurant I work at now. They were wonderful to wait on, they were funny, they were pleasant, and they left a 100 percent tip. They just doubled the bill. I've had a lot of celebrities, whose names will go unmentioned, who come in and leave 5 percent and think that's wonderful. They don't get it. I'm not sure if they don't care or if they don't know.

Ray Proscia
Georgia
West Hollywood, California

The customers are in control of the waitperson's salary. You give people this thimbleful of power after they've been kicked around by their boss, or their wife, or whoever's been bugging them all day, and they get drunk on that power and don't handle it very well.

Nancy Kelly
New York City

I have a pretty relaxed attitude about tipping; you take the good with the bad. At my restaurant they tend to overtip, so I have no complaints. One time in New York I dropped this check at a table and the tax had worked out to be $6.66. I asked the guy, "Are you superstitious?" and he said no. Then he left me $16.66 for a tip.

Michael K.
The Grill
Beverly Hills, California

Tipping can be a very intimidating thing for a person. I understand that. I've been on the other side, in various tipping situations. It can be very intimidating. But I think that, especially in a city like New York, they should know. And if they don't know, it should only take them once or twice to figure it out. Our salary is not in the price of the meal, and they have a responsibility to pay for the service. And the minimum they should leave is 15 percent. If there was nothing wrong with the service, if you got what you needed, you should tip 15 percent.

We're not there to be at their beck and call every second, that's not what it's about. We have other tables and they should have a life. They should be able to talk among themselves and not be constantly after a waiter. As soon as they start badgering you, you know they don't have a life; because it's not that important. If you're really hungry I'll bring you crudités, I'll bring you extra bread, but I don't have any control over what goes on in the kitchen so don't give me a hard time. Don't keep asking me when it will be ready; have a conversation with the person sitting across from you. I don't feel guilty about that, and I make it clear. I'll say, "I checked on it, it's coming," or, "It's backed up, it will be a few minutes." If they don't give me a hard time I'll buy them a round of drinks, but if they do, I could give a fuck. They should tip the minimum 15 percent. And if they were the least bit happy they should tip more. They will get better service.

> Freeda Kaufman
> Jethro's Bar & Grill
> New York City

It's an odd system here, because you don't get paid up front for waiting tables, you get paid after you do the work. And that is a totally demeaning position. With Americans there is a tacit understanding that they will pay you for the work done, but when you're dealing with Europeans it's a gamble whether or not you will get the money. You could be great and you'll get nothing. The only advantage we have with customers is that they're sitting lower than we are. It's that performer thing of imagining people in their underwear. If I'm having a bad night I just remember that I'm talking *down* to these people.

> Jennifer
> L'acajou
> New York City

When I worked in New Jersey I had a great customer who we called Beaver. That was his nickname. He would come in at 9:30 P.M. and he wanted everybody to serve him. He usually brought in different women that he wanted to show off. One night he came in by himself and I said, "Beaver, where's your date?" He said, "You're my date. You're going to sit down and eat with me." I said, "I can't, I'm working." So he talked to the boss and the boss said it was okay. We ordered two lobsters, wine, dessert, everything. We had a nice dinner and then I got tipped on top of the bill. It was the best.

> Jackie Becke
> Los Angeles, California

I don't look at my tips. I just can't bear to look at my tips. When I go out to eat I triple the tax for a tip, because it's the hardest work that I've ever done. And I've done other work. I feel bad for waiters. I've never met anyone who has waited tables for over three years who likes it.

My sister will chase you down and choke you with your Hermès scarf to get an extra dollar, but I can't do that. I figure that no matter how worked up I get over an individual tip I'm going to make the same amount at the end of the night. If you leave me a bad tip I don't want to talk to you, or look in your face. I'd rather you just walk out of the restaurant and get run over by a bus. And if you don't get run over today I'll just assume you'll get run over another day. If you don't tip properly you will die an untimely, painful death.

> Waiter X
> Khin Khao
> New York City

I don't have a problem with working for tips because basically that's what everyone does. I mean, agents work for tips—they live off percentages from their clients. And they have more attitude than anybody. I provide a service and people pay me for it. It's not all that different for doctors and lawyers. But people should tip more. There's something that should be put in every waiter's manual: when a customer says to you, at the end of a meal, "That was the best service I have ever received," you're going to get STIFFED! Guaranteed. When they say that to me, I run for the hills. Conversely, when I'm very busy, when I'm being particularly abusive or ignoring my customers, I always get a good tip. This leads me to belive that most people enjoy being treated like shit, and will pay through the nose for it.

Gregg Ostrin
Beverly Hills, California

America has a great history with slavery, and I think that even in a supposedly liberal city like New York people still have this psychological thing about paying someone to slave for them. I see it every night; people look at the bill not so much to see that the total of the bill is right, they do it to figure out how little they can get away with paying this person to slave on them. I really believe that. I'm not sure how conscious it is, but I think that subconsciously people resent having to pay someone to bring their food out.

It's funny because I'm Australian and my girlfriend grew up in the French part of Canada, and the worst tippers in the whole wide world are Australians and French Canadians. In Australia all the waiters get the minimum wage, which is six or seven dollars an hour now—a lot of money. Restaurants there are really struggling now, they can't afford to pay those kind of wages. And the thing about that is the general public knows they're getting paid so it's not so mandatory to tip. But wherever you go in the world you should learn the rules. I just find it amazing, even with out-of-towners who come into town, that they have no idea what the rule is. It gets back to this: in New York City you give 15 percent. This is the custom. It's just the way it has been worked out. I mean we don't make a great living being waiters. It's not bad; I make a decent living, but sometimes I wonder. For the amount of pressure and the expense of adrenaline I go through every night, is it worth it?

I've given up worrying about it, because what you lose on the swings you make up on the seesaw. You know what I'm saying? It's not worth it. You're under so much pressure the whole time that it's really not worth getting any more aggravated about people's meanness, or about their stupidity, or anything else. I always look at my tips, but the only time I'll ever say anything is if we get a large group of people and they haven't left you anything; you know, the check is $200 and they haven't left you a cracker. I'll go up and say to them, "Was the service all right? Because it's normal to leave some kind of gratuity in New York City, usually 15 percent." I don't know whether it's honest or not, but usually they will say something like, "Oh, we're sorry, it totally slipped our minds." But like I said, it's just not worth the aggravation.

It's a weird industry, because in just about every other profession you get paid before you get the goods. In corporate America you at least get some money down if it's a big contract. In a restaurant you don't pay until you have everything and you're on the way out the door. It's a very strange situation to be at the customer's mercy like that. I just think that wherever you are in the world you should know how to tip. Because in a sense it *is* prenegotiated. In New York City it's 15 percent, in Italy it's something else, but it's something you should know before you walk in the door because it is your responsibility to pay. I feel that I am providing a service and that people should recognize that I am providing a service. And that's the reason that people come to a restaurant in the first place; because they don't want to cook, because they want to go out, because they want to make some kind of social statement. But it comes back to the point that people don't want to pay for what they consider to be slave labor.

Chico Garcia
Midnight Lake
New York City

I think that for the most part, people don't base their tips on service. Most people tip 15 percent, no more. If I give especially good service, or do something out of the ordinary, I expect to get a better-than-average tip. Say, 20 percent. But that seldom happens. People really stick to 15 percent.

The last restaurant I worked at was in Boston and we had a clientele that was largely college students. Really young people coming in for cheap beer. This place had hundreds of different kinds of beer. Most of them were bad tippers. If somebody ordered a Mickey's Big Mouth, you *knew* you were going to get stiffed. A couple of nights a week we had free food at midnight, and these kids would come in for free food and Mickey's Big Mouth. It was a bummer.

Kelsey Geisler
Trompe L'oeil
New York City

I used to work at a restaurant where we didn't pool tips, and now I work at a restaurant where we do. I like pooling tips. There is more incentive for the staff to work together to get the job done. Previously I always worried about who I had to wait on. We always talked about the difference between suits and skirts. What it came down to was who was getting the suits and who was getting the skirts. Men will come in and order more food; they'll order steaks, and women will order salads. So if you waited on the women you would make a lot less money. And you also had to worry about whether the host liked you or not. If the host is pissed off at you, they won't seat your station.

The worst thing that can happen with regard to tipping is when somebody writes, "Terrible service," on the credit card slip. That has happened to me twice. But I would have to say that for the most part I get tipped pretty well.

Dan Shapero
San Francisco, California

It's funny how much of the world walking around out there seems to think that tipping is just sort of an option. They don't realize that we pretty much work for tips; that we get shit for pay, that we get no benefits, and that it's not only physically demanding, but it's *emotionally* demanding. When you have somebody who is pleasant waiting on you in a restaurant it can make your dining experience. At almost all of the restaurants I have worked in, you were not allowed to say anything to people who didn't tip you adequately. And it's outrageous what people will try to get away with. Not just a party of two; I'm talking about a party of ten with a huge tab leaving less than 10 percent on the bill. It's insulting. One time I did follow a guy out the door. He left me pennies and nickels and dimes on the table, and I scraped them into my hand and went running out behind him and I said, "Here, I think you need these a little more than I do." I don't think he got it—he was totally stunned. I guess a lot of people don't take time to think about it. They don't understand, or they don't care.

Bridget Munger
Arthur's Landing
Weehawken, New Jersey

When I first started I felt uncomfortable with the whole idea of getting money directly from customers, as if a paycheck was earned but this was like a handout. I'm still unable to chase after tables that don't leave good tips, and I get a little queasy saying thank you so much. I do get a kick out of the people who come over and hand me their tips and say, "This is for you, honey. Buy yourself something pretty."

Cherie Hamblin
Moondance Diner
New York City

Tipping is a weird thing. When I go out to eat, I'm always throwing down. But some people just don't do it. To some people a $10 tip seems like a lot of money. But if the check is $200 they need to understand that $10 is *way* light, and they should un-ass some more money.

I was waiting on these sorority girls in Austin once. If you have never been to Texas, I can tell you what the Greek system is all about there: they all suck. They are basically the kind of people who don't give a shit about anybody else; they're just living off of Mommy and Daddy's money. So they had like $40 worth of margaritas and left me a pile of change on the table for a tip. And I just wasn't going to stand for it this time; it killed me. So I walked out the door and threw the pile of change out behind them. They called me a fuckhead and left, but I got my satisfaction because I let them know I didn't need their chicken scratch.

Dickie Mallison
MacArthur Park
San Francisco, California

Well, I never realized, because I came from Las Vegas, where you make a lot of money and then you get tips too, how important tipping is. In Florida you don't make money; you just get tips. I had never experienced that. In Florida you get $2 an hour. When I left Vegas seven years ago you made $6.50 an hour, plus tips. It's ridiculous. It makes for bad employee morale. When I would clean and straighten up at a restaurant in Florida, the other waitresses would say, "Beck, what are you doing that for? You're going to make us look bad." I like to clean, what can I tell you? I hate to stand around.

I've had some awesome tips. I've had a table of four

leave me $200. This was in Nantuckett. I don't compare anything with Nantuckett, because in Nantuckett we made big, big, big money. I used to wait on Mr. Johnson and Johnson once a week. He'd leave me $75 for three of them. He was very generous, and so polite. He's not pretentious at all either. He's incredible. He always said thank you. It surprises you when somebody does that because in general people are so rude. I had a regular named Mr. Crabb, who owns an antique store on Nantuckett. Once a week he'd come in and leave me $75. He just loved me.

In Vegas it was different. The customers hate you because they lost all their money.

Becky Milici
Fama
Santa Monica, California

Sometimes the idea of waiting on people for money seems sort of strange. It seems degrading somehow. But then again, sometimes the idea of going out to eat in a restaurant seems weird; that you're going to this building where strangers are going to prepare food with their hands for you to eat. I feel that people don't realize that we do work for tips. Like with elderly people, you get 10 percent if you're lucky. I don't think they know that we don't get paid by the restaurant. Also, Europeans don't tip. I mean, we all know what to do when we go to Europe; you read the guide book and it tells you how much to tip. I can't believe that their guide books don't tell them how to tip in the USA. That false ignorance doesn't work for me.

Stacey Jurewicz
Pescatore
New York City

Europeans don't tip!

Dimitri Rathschech
New York City

I used to feel that tipping was an option. I suppose in the strictest sense it is; it's a gratuity, a gift. However, now that the government is taxing us on a percentage of the checks we write, and assuming that we're being tipped at a certain rate, my feeling is that if you can't afford to tip don't come in my restaurant. Go to McDonald's if you don't want to tip. I had this one table, a nice young couple, and we were having a great time. I had a great rapport with them—we were laughing, and I usually don't have a great rapport with guests because I despise them from the second I walk up to the table. They had a great time. When they left the busboy came up to me and said, "They didn't like you very much did they?" and I said, "No, they liked me fine," and he shows me this bread plate that has a handful of pennies and nickels in it. They paid the check and just jammed out the door. I was so mad, and so violated, that I went over to the table to see if maybe some money had blown off the table onto the floor. No. But he left this $300 leather jacket there. I said, "Gimme that thing!" and grabbed it out of the busboy's hand. I knew he was going to have to come back for it. So I see him, he's crawling back up the stairs toward me. I didn't say anything, I was just watching him squirm. He said, "You know, I left my leather jacket. And hey, we didn't leave you enough tip." I said, "Really? *I didn't notice*. I didn't notice that you *dumped out the bottom of your purse as my damn tip*." So he handed me $15 on a $30 check, and I said, "Now you can have your jacket back."

Doug V.
Los Angeles, California

If a customer leaves me a bad tip I always nail them. I go up to the table and say, "Was everything all right?" and they'll say, "Yeah," and I'll ask, "So you had a good time tonight?" and they'll say, "Yeah." And then I'll say, "Well, I was curious; why did you only leave me $5 on a $75 check?" Then they'll say, "The kitchen was slow."

And I'll say, "That's not my fault, is it?" and they'll say
something like, "Well, it was slow service," to which I will
respond, "No, it was just a shitty tip."

I want 20 percent. That's it. I deserve it. I won't accept
anything less than 15 percent. And another thing: *I remember the faces.* I will not wait on somebody who
doesn't know how to tip. If you leave me a lousy tip
don't come back in here and expect me to wait on you.
Maybe one of the other waiters will, but I won't.

Europeans don't tip. And the other kiss of death is
when someone stands up and says, "That was great service, great service." It's gonna be 8 percent.

> Ted LoRusso
> Perretti's
> New York City

The bad-tipping regular, that's the worst. If the guy
comes in and doesn't tip and you never see him again
that's okay—you get over it. But if you have to see the
asshole day after day, or every week . . .

> Eileen Schwartz
> West Lynn Cafe
> Austin, Texas

It's just part of the game for me, getting bad tips. I
don't get that excited when I get a great tip, and I don't
get that down when I get a bad one. The customers have
us in a bad position, and in a way we have them in a bad
position. It's the way the system is set up. The only way
we're rewarded is through a tip. We don't work to im-
press our managers; we're not going to get promotions,
we don't get raises, and we're never going to get a pat on
the back. We work to get tips. That's just the way the
thing is set up, and I don't have a problem with it. What
other relationship in the job world is as objective as
that? Granted you're at the mercy of the person with the
pen in their hand, but it's been my experience that if
you're a good waiter you're going to make more money

than a mediocre waiter, and a bad waiter is not going to make very much at all.

Garrett Harker
San Francisco, California

I don't mind working for tips because I know what I do is very damn good. The only time working for tips is a drag is when you're waiting on Europeans. And it pisses me off because they seem to read the entire tour guide book except for the tip page. For some reason they skip that page. We get a lot of Europeans in this restaurant. The other night I had a guy leave me $3 on a $100 check and I asked him to take it back. He asked me why and I told him it was really, really lousy. He was German, but he lives here now; so there was really no excuse. I know what I do at a table, I know what my service is worth. But I'd much rather work for tips than for $8 an hour or something, because that sucks.

I hate working for tips if the other waiter is bad, because then I'm working my ass off and they're getting shit tips all night long. But that's because we pool tips. I would hate to work in a nonpool house because then you have to worry about who you're waiting on, and who has seniority; it's really fucked. In a situation like that the other waiter can be making $200 the same night that you make $80. It's fucked up. Nobody helps each other—it's very bad.

Gary Chiappa
Roettele A.G.
New York City

Here's a typical situation where people will undertip. A couple will bring in kids and feed them Cheerios. First of all, you're stuck with a deuce at a four-top because they will have a high chair. And they feed this kid Cheerios. There are Cheerios flying everywhere, and they don't understand that you, the waiter, have to clean the mess up. So they just leave a normal tip. They should leave you like 25 percent.

This is in the same category: a regular that tries to be-friend you and tips badly, thinking that his friendliness is some sort of a tip. They want to know about everything that you do ... I have no idea what these people are thinking. If people are rude to you you will make a whole lot more money. Because people will realize, sometimes they will realize, that they have been rude. You haven't fucked up and they were still rude to you, and they'll real-ize by the end of the meal, well, he took a lot of shit. He took a lot of shit and he's still standing.

See, that's what it all comes down to; the biggest of all pet peeves: people who don't tip enough. Because that is all that it is about. It's all about a dollar.

Lars Goransson
Austin, Texas

Taxes

All waiters and waitresses pay their fair share of income tax. We declare every penny we make in tips. Honest. Okay?

Dating

Waiting tables is a great way to meet people. Most of my friends in New York are people who I have worked with on the floor of a restaurant, or people I have waited on. I have often thought that if I had a real job and were transferred to a new city, I would work a couple of nights a week in a restaurant until I built a circle of friends.

The reasons why restaurants are a great place to meet people are manifest; first of all, lots of people come through the doors. Secondly, people tend to let their guard down a bit when they go out to eat; the lights are low, the booze is flowing, and they are there to enjoy themselves. Also, when people find a restaurant they like they come back again and again. A good restaurant can be very much like a clubhouse in this way, with familiar faces around the room every night. Not too surprisingly, romance, or at least lust, frequently blooms in such a fertile environment.

As a waiter I have seen countless men and women come to a restaurant without a date and leave with one, or with telephone numbers exchanged and the intention of meeting again in the future. And truth be told, I have dated quite a few of my customers. Businesswise, I think this is probably a bad idea because you run the risk of losing a customer if things go poorly. But personally, it works out well.

I think you can learn a great deal about someone by how they behave in a restaurant. Table manners alone speak volumes. Call me Judith Martin, but I don't want to go out with someone who chews with their mouth open, smokes while I'm still eating, or holds their fork in a fist while they cut their steak. Also, if someone is mean to waiters, they're probably just plain mean. So by waiting on a woman I can usually determine if I would like to get to know her better. Similarly, if a woman comes into the restaurant several times she will have the opportunity to figure out that I'm not a complete psycho, or that I am and she knows what she's in for.

It is also not uncommon for waiters and waitresses to date each other (and by extension, waiters date waiters, and waitresses date waitresses). As in every other business, this can be disastrous. But stories abound. And for every couple that lives happily ever after, there are countless people who have to get new jobs. Every time I find myself becoming attracted to someone I work with I tighten my belt a notch tighter and repeat, "Don't fish in the company pond," until the sensation goes away. Life is too short. Of course, I haven't always been this sage; I once moved in with a waitress I was working with after our first date. But that was a long time and several jobs ago. I should add that I have nothing against dating waitresses, they are generally very bright, funny, captivating people. I just don't think people who work with each other should become romantically involved. Or they should do it with their eyes wide open and the next job lined up.

I asked the people I interviewed if they had ever dated a customer. Some said they had and told me about the dates, others shared their views on the subject, and still others told of dating people they worked with. Here's what waiters and waitresses said about trying to find love in a restaurant.

Have I ever dated a customer? I married one. Ian Astbury, the lead singer from the Cult, came in to Mel n' Rose's with his girlfriend and this other little guy one morning when I was working. They were all in full gear at nine o'clock. All the waitresses were swooning over Ian and I said, "I kind of like that little hard-looking dude." So I married him. My maiden name was Cara Brown, his name is Tim Green. No kidding.

> Cara Green
> Swingers
> Los Angeles, California

I dated a customer once and he took me for $2,000.

> Alexandra Lee
> New York City

I think dating customers is a bad idea—it's shitting where you eat.

> Bob Dombrowski
> Orso
> New York City

It seems that the staff dates each other more than their customers. I had never dreamed of dating a customer before I met my last boyfriend; it was much more fun to have secret crushes. Regulars are a big thing at the diner and Leo worked across the street so he came in every day. We had known each other for a year or so before we had the nerve to date. I guess I thought of him as more staff than customer, but the dating thing was still delicate—fighting in the restaurant, tension, etc. I once shot a loaf of bread across the table at Leo and told him to get out (he did and I blushed for the rest of the day). We dated for two years and it was easier to break up with him when he started working somewhere else.

By the way, I am amazed at the misunderstandings that arise from being nice to customers. Male customers are forever mistaking kindness for genuine, datelike interest, and it is really uncomfortable—they know where you are and you're trapped. A customer who wouldn't leave me alone once tied flowers to my bike, which was parked outside, with a big sign that said, "I love you, Cherie," and I didn't realize why everyone was smiling at me until I went to go home.

Cherie Hamblin
Moondance Diner
New York City

A friend of mine works at a restaurant in West Holly-wood, which is a very gay part of town. When he dropped the check at this one table one of the guys left a deposit slip with the money on the table. The point being that it had his name, address, and telephone number on it. My friend wasn't interested so he went back to the table and said, "Rex? Are you Rex? Are you making a deposit? Because this branch is closed."

Doug V.
Los Angeles, California

I would never date a customer. I never have. I hate customers.

Shawna Mason
Lone Star Roadhouse
New York City

I've had sex with a lot of customers, but never really dated them or necessarily knew their names, or ever even saw them again. I think it's fine. I think it keeps them coming back.

Gary Chiappa
Roettele A.G.
New York City

I'm dating a waitress now, but I have dated customers. I've noticed that female waiters get hit on all the time by men, and male waiters get hit on all the time by men also. It's rare that women will proposition a waiter. I used to find, when I worked in Venice, that Sunday brunch was the best time to pick up women and I did it left, right, and center. I dated this beautiful German therapist for a while but it became too much work; I had to bring the ink blots all the time. She came in with one of the owners one time and it was a little uncomfortable. But I've never lost a customer.

> Gregg Ostrin
> Beverly Hills, California

I've fucked customers. Dating implies a process, like more than once.

> Waiter X
> Khin Khao
> New York City

I dated a customer once. It turned out to be a bad thing because the guy was a jerk. But I don't think that had anything to do with the fact that he was my customer. It's a very rare thing that a guy will make a pass at me at work. The only time a guy will make a pass at me is when he's with a woman and she's paying, and then I don't make any money.

> Jennifer
> L'acajou
> New York City

You have to really be careful when you date a customer. It's not a great idea. It's not good for business. You can lose a customer and it can make your life complicated. On the other hand, you learn a lot about a person very quickly in a restaurant environment. I met my boyfriend Brad waiting on him. I was attracted to him because he came by himself, and I've always had a problem going to restaurants by myself. I get a little paranoid, wondering what people are thinking about why I'm by myself. I could see that Brad was totally independent and comfortable with himself. He knew what he wanted to order, and he *always* knew what he wanted to drink.

He was very polite and no trouble. So I became attracted to him.

> Freeda Kaufman
> Jethro's Bar & Grill
> New York City

I have never dated a customer, but I would if he tipped me really well and left his number on the check.

> Malika Simmons
> Around The Clock
> New York City

You've got to have a schtick. I mean you can't go in there and be who you really are. That's why the relationships I've had with people who knew me as a waiter have been so disastrous.

> Mark Collins
> Universal Grill
> New York City

I don't think it's a good idea to date customers. I'll have fun with them, but I won't date them. I have a friend, I won't mention his name, and he went out with a woman he waited on. She seemed normal, but she turned out to be a wacko. She kept calling him, and calling him, and calling him, and calling him; she wouldn't leave him alone.

> Pietro Bottero
> The Dock
> Fire Island, New York

Yes, I have dated customers. But there is no great story. And the fact that they know where to find you can be a bit suffocating.

> Robin Maynor
> Linn's Fruit Bin
> Cambria, California

I worked at a little beach bar in Florida that was open from 10:00 A.M. to 7:00 P.M. One of my customers was the president of a local bank and he always wanted to date me. My policy was to never date the customers because you can lose them. He was very insistent. Since I wouldn't go out with him, one night he brought a chef and food for twenty people and we all had dinner together after the place closed. Needless to say, I did accept a date after that. For dinner he took me to Belize, Central America, where we ate fresh chicken that we had watched being killed, plucked, and cooked. But there is no happy ending to the story. He wasn't the guy for me.

Rose Larsen
Rose's Den at the Boulder Inn
Milepost 28, Highway 93
Kingman, Arizona

I've dated customers plenty of times. Not only the customers, but waiters and chefs, too. When you spend 90 percent of your time at work, that's where you meet people. Most of the time it has been really good friendships that developed into something else.

I did date a chef I worked with. It was interesting because we were set up by his ex-wife, who is friends with his current girlfriend also. And he and I are still friends to this day.

There have been some bad mistakes made, when I just see somebody and then I meet them after work. And the next thing I know I'm making out with them in a bathroom somewhere.

A restaurant is a great place to meet people. Some people I know swear that they will not go out with anybody they meet at work. But customers are just people like anybody else.

Julie Marr
Orson's
New York City

I would date a customer, of course. But I doubt that I would date anyone who comes into *this* restaurant. The clientele is the thirty-plus crowd who have money, or think they have money, or wish they had money; it's just not my crowd. Some people have tried to go out with me, friends of the owner's, but I said no. When I worked at Sunset Grill and Bar, in Boston, I used to get asked out a lot. It's like, how could they not like you? Here you are: you're nice, you're smiling, and you're bringing them food.

Kelsey Geisler
Trompe L'oeil
New York City

The girl from Georgia who I was going to marry was a customer at Benny's. She came in and left me her phone number, and I went out with her that night, and for the next two and a half years after that. We got engaged and everything. I was going to marry her and then last year we broke up. This year I dated this girl named Bailey, this rich Upper West Side girl. She was going to fly me to France—her father is totally loaded. So I lived the Upper West Side lifestyle for a while. I stayed in her apartment, it was huge and she had bought it, and she was going to fly me to France, but I started to feel weird about the prospect of her paying for everything so I kind of backed off. I've dated customers, and I'm constantly looking. Me and the manager I work with now, we're both horndogs, and the night's not complete unless we get a beautiful girl in there. I'll say, "See the girl on thirty-five?" and he'll say, "Oh my God." And it's even gotten to the point where I'll say, "thirty-five," and he knows exactly what I'm talking about.

Russell Dean Anderson
Miracle Grill
New York City

I have never dated a customer and I am surprised because I'm pretty damn handsome. Maybe my incompetence as a waiter has something to do with it, or perhaps they think everything will be cold by the time I'm ready to serve.

Sam K.
Rox
Beverly Hills, California

I have, on various occasions, dated customers. It never works out (not that other relationships do) because they expect me to be the same charming character that I am at work.

Sebastion Elliot
The Riviera
New York City

I have dated several customers, and each time it happens I say that it will never happen again. Then a week later some Betty walks in the door and knocks me backward and I'm going out with her. It's bad because most of the time it's just one less customer who will be coming back to the restaurant. Because I know I'm going to fuck it up somehow. I've had my fellow employees say, "Don't do it," because they know how it's going to work out.

Dickie Mallison
MacArthur Park
San Francisco, California

Food

If there is one area of my job where I really fall down, it is representing the products that I sell. A waiter's job, from the customer's perspective, is to make them feel welcome and serve what they order when they want it. From the restaurant's perspective, a waiter's job is to make the customers feel welcome, and sell them as much food and drink as possible. So on one level we are truly salespeople.

To perform well as a salesperson, one must be knowledgeable and enthusiastic about the product one is trying to sell. I am admittedly inadequate in this area. Fortunately, food is unlike other products. When someone walks into a clothing store or an automobile dealership, there is no guarantee that they will buy anything—they might just be looking for the best price or comparison shopping. When someone sits down at a table in a restaurant you can be fairly sure they are going to order a meal.

My problem is that I don't care about, or even like, the food I sell. I work in a restaurant with a continental menu. We serve steaks, seafood, poultry, pasta, and that sort of thing. I can tell by looking that the food probably tastes good, but I won't eat any of it. I am a vegetarian. I don't eat red meat, fish, or poultry, and I try to avoid dairy. I don't drink alcoholic beverages either. As a result, when somebody asks me how something is I'm never really sure what to say. I suppose it ultimately doesn't matter, because if you say an item is great the customer will invariably reply, "Oh, I bet you say that about everything." But it does make me uncomfortable, because as a rule, I don't like to lie. So I will usually tell my customers that the item they have asked me about looks really good and that everyone else who has ordered it seems to like it. When they say, "You haven't tried it?" I tell them, truthfully, that since our menu changes every week, and there are different specials every night, that it is impossible to taste everything.

Why, you might ask, don't I work in a vegetarian restaurant? Because most vegetarian restaurants are much less expensive than the restaurant I work in, and many don't serve alcohol. Alcohol increases your check totals, and since we work for a percentage of what we sell, it is in my best interest to work in a moderately expensive restaurant.

But food seems to be a prickly issue for many people these days. It seems that at every table I walk up to there is someone who gives me an order that sounds like this, "I'd like a house salad, dressing on the side. No, make that no dressing—just bring me vinegar and oil. The chicken, is it on the bone? What is it, a boneless breast? Okay, I'd like that. There's no skin is there? Okay, I'll have that. Is it grilled? No? Can they grill it? Okay, but no butter. And no oil. The vegetables, can they just steam them? Make *sure* there's no butter or oil, I can't have *any* butter or oil." Our checks look like novels now. I've actually thought about writing to the people who print them and asking if they will add about a foot to the length of the checks just to accommodate the preponderance of special orders. I pity the waiters who have to use computers, they have to type in so many modifiers they risk getting carpal tunnel syndrome every shift. And the question on every waiter's mind is, why don't these people go someplace where they make food the way they like it?

Another problem area is food "allergies." Everyone is "allergic" to some kind of food now. I use quotation marks because I have a hard time accepting that food allergies are so common. I mean, it's widely known that a small percentage of the human race are fatally allergic to some kinds of nuts. There is scientific documentation of this. But if we, as a species, suffer as much food allergy as I am presented with every night at work, we will most surely be starved into extinction in the near future. As an example, I recently waited on a woman who handed me a laminated card that listed fifteen food items that would cause a fatal allergic reaction. I cannot tell you the difficulties this presented. In my restaurant, the executive chef creates the sauces and recipes in the daytime and the cooks simply heat these things and put them all together at night. We have no way of knowing all the ingredients of some of the dishes. I spent literally thirty minutes negotiating between this woman and the kitchen to create a meal that would not *kill* her. Suffice to say, her party did not think this was any extra service and left me a 15 percent tip. I did tell her that I was as uncomfortable holding her life in my hands as she should be having me hold it. And the question here was, why would someone with this type of health concern ever eat out?

One thing is for certain, the better the food that your restaurant serves, the easier your job is as a waiter. There is nothing as disheartening as serving people bad food. And it creates infinitely more work—if a customer doesn't like something you have to discuss it with them and determine if they want it taken off the check or if they want to order something different. In either case you have to talk to the manager and the chef, and the less of this you do, the happier you generally are. And, of course, it is usually the waiter who suffers. Because if somebody doesn't like their food, they almost always leave a bad tip. *As if.* As if the waiter cooked it.

On the other hand, if your restaurant serves great food the customers are happy and they love you. It's that simple.

Beverages are a hoot to me. Wine in particular. I know nothing about wine, but I can fake it. I just read the descrip-

tion from the *Wine Spectator*. And that's where the fun be-
gins. *Flavors of oak, cherry, and plum*. Hello! Have you seen
the emperor's new clothes? Here's my rule of thumb: the
more someone pays for a bottle of wine, the more they will
enjoy it. Call me crazy, but it's true. Beer and spirits are
much easier—people know what they like, they order it, they
never complain about it, and your check totals go up, up, up.
But there are ethical dilemmas. Do you continue to serve
someone who is visibly drunk (the law says no, the owner
says yes)? And what about a pregnant woman? I seem to remember two waiters being fired in Oregon for refusing to
serve one. The management position seems to be like any
other business: if you can squeeze one more dollar out of
them, do it.

When I met with a waiter or a waitress, I simply asked them
to talk about the food they served. I didn't want to limit the
discussion in any way. This is what they said.

I feel good about most of the stuff I serve. And I'll
be honest if something on the menu is not good. But I
just eat to eat, and I still don't get how people plan a
whole night and make this event out of eating. To me,
you eat like you go to the bathroom, you just do it to
live.

> Bob Dombroski
> Orso
> New York City

I worked at the Empire Diner for two weeks, and the
only shift I could get was the graveyard shift, which was
from midnight to eight o'clock in the morning. Weird
place. The food was really bad, the clientele was horrible. The most interesting part was that at about four or
five o'clock the street bums would come in and ask for a
cup of soup or something, and they were the nicest people who would come in. But their food was free. We'd get
a lot of people coming in after they'd been out partying
somewhere else and usually by that time they'd be to-

tally obnoxious. You'd ask if everything was all right and they would say it was fine because they just couldn't get it together mentally to send it back. I lasted two weeks, and then told them to forget it.

I waited tables at two places in Australia, one a big hotel where I worked part-time as a wine waiter. I was eighteen years of age and had just started university. I learned about wine on the job. I was young and spunky and they hired me. The only thing the manager told me was that all red wines are dry; so if anyone asked for a dry red wine I wasn't going to be in any trouble. Eventually he worked through the different kinds of wine on the list. I mean, most people don't know what they're drinking anyway.

People have a psychological barrier toward food. They don't even want it to look like food anymore. They're so frightened by what they read in the magazines about the pollution in the rivers and the different kinds of insecticides that are used in the fields, and the lead pollution in the water, and the mercury in the ocean. I mean they're taught as kids about the basic food groups that are good for them, and they're taught as adults about everything that is bad.

I think McDonald's has got it sewn up. It's got the formula down perfectly. First of all, they have this hamburger patty that has been minced up so much that it doesn't even look like meat. I mean, they could change it even more but then it would become a parody of itself. It's on these buns that look nothing like a classic piece of bread. It has these funny bits of vegetable on it that look more like tepid pieces of performance art than anything nourishing. They even give you just the right amount of ketchup on your burger. The cheese is so full of food dye that it's totally unrecognizable as anything else except a covering so you can't see anything. It's so soft and malleable that it can be masticated by everything from gummy four-month-old babies to gummy ninety-seven-year-old great-grandparents. And the great thing about McDonald's is that they don't have waiters.

Chico Garcia
Midnight Lake
New York City

One of the things I have noticed—Isabella's was like this, and my last job was like this—is that they will feed you a staff meal that is repellant and then expect you to go out and sell what is on the menu. I mean, last week's shit, and it would be old and half the staff would have an upset stomach. It's like, what are they trying to do, send the whole staff to the hospital? It's because they don't want to spend one extra penny feeding the staff. A lot of owners and managers have this attitude that the staff is like disposable cattle. I once told a manager, "You treat us like toilet paper; rip it off, use it, and throw it out." That's the approach a lot of places take.

Bridget Munger
Arthur's Landing
Weehawken, New Jersey

I worked at The Good Earth, it's this pseudo health-food restaurant. There were these two women who used to come in, a daughter and a mother. One time the daughter says, "Instead of the rolls you bring out, I want tortillas. I want you to bring me a side of lettuce, which I know you don't charge for, a side of salsa, which I know you don't charge for, a side of tomatoes, which I know you don't charge for, and some beans." So basically this whole feast was going to cost $1.95, the price of a side of beans. I just stopped writing and said, "I'm sorry, this is not the Salvation Army soup kitchen, we are not in business to give away food. If you need help there's a place to go for food stamps." They went through the roof. I said, "Do you understand that we want to be accommodating, but we can't stay in business if we give away the food?"

Doug V.
Los Angeles, California

I worked at The Seaport, at the South Street Seaport, for about twenty minutes. The food there was just embarrassing. Everything was breaded. It was a fish restaurant and all the fish was breaded. All the dishes were a tiny piece of fish with about a pound of fried breading around it. It was just too embarrassing. And you had to wear white jeans, so you walked around with grease spots all night.

Shawna Mason
Lone Star Roadhouse
New York City

I worked in a vegetarian restaurant so I had all these particular people. And they are so smug about it, like they are *so* healthy. This restaurant I work at, a lot of people have this impression that it's a health-food restaurant because it's vegetarian. We have all these desserts, and all of our desserts have sugar and eggs in them. The customers will say, "Why don't you have anything healthy?" and it's like, oh *excuse me,* I didn't realize your pasta dish, with ten ounces of olive oil, and five pounds of cheese, was a health-food dish, and that you would want something dairyless and sugarless for dessert. Go pull a rope.

Eileen Schwartz
West Lynn Cafe
Austin, Texas

Food has major psychological implications. As a waiter you are faced with the impact of how their parents fed them. If food was withheld, or used as a reward, and so forth. They come here and *we* are their mommies and daddies. You can tell exactly how a person was raised by *how* they order food. It's not so much what they order, but how they order it. A pampered person, Miss Thing, comes in and says, "I want this, but I want it this way," and you know that Miss Thing got her way from her daddy her whole life, and now I have to do it for her. So it is fun to say, "I can't do that," just to see the look on her face.

To the customers, a menu is a blueprint, a list of ingredients, and they feel that they can just go for it, make it into whatever they want. They don't understand that it is the way it is, that the chef has designed it that way, and that he doesn't want to make things differently. This society gives too many people the permission to be creative.

Also, people don't order food anymore. If I have a party of fifteen coming in, I know that they aren't all going to order a meal. It's going to be fifteen diet Cokes, seven salads, three bowls of pasta, and fifteen separate checks. Plus, half of them will have shown up late and I'll have to be ordering from the kitchen all night long. I always want to ask them, "What would you say to me if I showed up to a dinner party at your house an hour and a half late and told you to go back in the kitchen and make me some food now?"

> Ted LoRusso
> Perretti's
> New York City

Here's a typical situation. Yesterday I served a pasta dish, mushroom fettuccine, to a customer and he says, "This is *it*? Your portions should be bigger." What can you do? I told him it is very filling, and he said, "Your portions are too small." But that's the thing, his first reaction was *you*. Let's think about this. My job is to pick up the food and bring it to the customer. I don't plan the menu, I don't determine the size of the dish, I don't cook the food, and I don't determine the price. But the main thing was, he was rude. If he had been nice I might have been inclined to do something.

> Becky Milici
> Fama
> Santa Monica, California

A lot of times people ask me my opinion about the food and I'm very straightforward. I tell them that the menu is great but that the steak sucks. It's a shitty cut of meat, so no matter how nice the cognac cream is, the steak sucks. But then I've worked in places when you put down a burger with fries and you run. I prefer to work in places where the food is fine. Fine meaning very, very good without being four star and having the environment that goes with that. I hate bow ties, I hate that sort of shit. I hate vests. I've always had a gut; there's nothing worse than a gut when you're wearing a fucking vest.

> Gary Chiappa
> Roettele A.G.
> New York City

I've worked in all kinds of places. When you can't serve good food you serve good attitude. The last restaurant I worked in was scummy. You just deal with it. Food presents difficult problems, like when somebody wants to send something back. Especially if there's nothing wrong with it. It's that okay-the-customer's-always-right-even-though-they're-starving-in-Somalia-we'll-throw-your-steak-out-and-get-you-a-new-one thing. My feeling is that if you want me to throw your food out, it'd better be because you found a finger in it. But if you work in an expensive place it's not like that. It's sorry, sorry, we're happy to waste valuable food for your caprice.

> Waiter X
> Khin Khao
> New York City

Every place I have worked has had some food that I didn't like and that I thought was bad. I always just push the better food. If someone orders something that I don't think is particularly good I tell them to order something else. And I think people appreciate that honesty.

> Jackie Becke
> Los Angeles, California

I worked in this restaurant, Josephina's, which was a pizza restaurant. They would have football night on

Monday night and the cocktail waitress would just get swamped. We would all try to help her, but she would just get swamped. You know, they would drink and drink, and order pizza after pizza. Anyway, you know how they have those rubber mats on the floor behind a bar? One time I saw her drop a pizza facedown onto the mat, and she just flipped the mat over so the pizza was back in its pan and went and served it.

Maryanne Contreras
Los Angeles, California

It's easier to get a drink order out of somebody in the age of sobriety than it is to get a dessert order out of people in the age of low fat and low cholesterol. I'll go up to a table and they'll say, "What have you got for dessert?" and I tell them everything we have for dessert. Then I usually try to say I'll be right back, or I immediately try to change the conversation to, "Who wants coffee?" because they begin this, "Will you split something with me?" Nobody ever eats a whole dessert anymore, you know? Nobody. It's "Will you split something with me? What do you think about this? What do you think about that?" And all the people are sitting around the table saying, "I don't know." It's like, are they going to be able to tell the person on the StairMaster next to them that they had a piece of apple pie last night? They're really ashamed of it. They'll order shots of tequila with no thought about tomorrow, but not dessert.

Mark Collins
Universal Grill
New York City

I worked with this chef named Dave who was a great cook. He would make us these amazing staff meals and then he would tell us the specials for the evening. There would be all these specials with about twelve ingredients each. He'd go into all this detail and I'd have to stop him and say, "Dave, what does it taste like?" and he'd say, "Good." That's all I need to know. I'd go out and sell the shit out of them.

> Matt Jaroszewicz
> Gainesville, Florida

In Wisconsin I worked at a place called Brat n' Brau. I had to wear a little brown polyester dress and a bonnet. I'm a vegetarian, and it was the biggest meat joint in town. It was meat, meat, meat, meat.

> Kelsey Geisler
> Trompe L'oeil
> New York City

I worked at this place in New York where you would have to put the food down and run, it was so bad. And then I worked at Chumley's for a while, where the food was also pretty bad, and I was waiting on these guys and they were all complaining. This one guy said that it looked like someone had taken a bite out of his pickle. I said, "Okay, everybody complain right now, let's get it all over with."

> Michael K.
> The Grill
> Beverly Hills, California

Rakel was on Varick and Clarkson in New York City, and it was voted, for two years in a row, one of the top-ten restaurants in the United States by two different magazines: *Gourmet* and *Food and Wine.* Anyway, there was this dish, and supposedly it is a classic French dish . . . only the French could eat something like this . . . it's an egg, and it's just about to hatch so there's a baby chick inside. So he cooks it, but not a lot, and I can't remember exactly what he did to it, maybe just boiled it for thirty seconds, but then he'd lop off the top of it and put the sauce in it. Then we would carry it out to the person, the unfortunate person who was about to eat it, while another waiter would have to come up and put a tablecloth over the customer's head and the dish so the other guests wouldn't have to see. It was just disgusting. I mean, it was a formed chicken embryo, and it was close to being raw, and they would eat the whole thing.

Michael Marx
Jethro's Bar & Grill
New York City

We had some awful food at Broadway Bay. People would ask me for recommendations or ask me if something was good, which I hate. I mean, obviously somebody thinks it is good or it wouldn't be on the menu. And it was a weird thing. Sometimes I wouldn't recommend something and people would look at me like they were pissed off because I wasn't saying what they wanted to hear and they had already decided that they were going to order that. A woman once stiffed me because I had recommended something and she didn't like it. I took it off the check and she stiffed me anyway. It's funny when you think the food in your restaurant is awful. We began to feel like the characters in "Alice," you know, talking about Mel's Diner. But there would be people in there eating and thinking it was good and coming back for more.

I was surprised to find out how many people don't know much about cooking processes. We served lobsters at Broadway Bay, which opened up a whole set of problems. I'd have to ask people if they wanted them steamed or broiled and many people would say, "What's the difference?" The only answer I could ever think of for that was, "Well, one is steamed and one is broiled." Lobsters molt, and when the shell is new it turns that bright red color that you think of when you see a cooked lobster, but if it has a thick shell it doesn't get bright red, it stays almost black or dark green. I served one of these steamed thick-shelled lobsters to a woman once and she called me over and said, "You can even *see* it's burnt!" I had to say to her, "Ma'am, food cooked in water doesn't turn black—you could cook it all week and it wouldn't turn black. It's a dark lobster shell." She wouldn't have it, I had to take it back. Or people would discover the tamale, the liver, for the first time. They'd see this green slime, that's what it is, but it's supposed to be a delicacy, and freak out, say it's a bad lobster and send it back. I got into an argument about that with an old man once. I had been working at this seafood restaurant for more years than I care to divulge, and he said, "Young lady, I have seen more lobsters in my life than you have," and I said, "Sir, you couldn't possibly have seen more lobsters than I have."

Oh yeah, whoever invented on-the-side should be executed at dawn. One of the waiters complained to me that it's mostly a female thing. Check it out, it's really only women who ask for things on the side. I think they have trouble relinquishing control. Food is their domain, and they can't just relax and let you bring something the way it's prepared, they have to have a hand in it. The dressing has to be on the side, but I'll watch them pick up the monkey dish and pour the *entire contents* onto the salad. And you had to balance the thing on your wrist, and somebody else has to bus it, and then somebody has to wash it. It's all unnecessary.

After a while I started to feel the way Lenin felt—you can't give people a choice. It's just too much for them to handle. You tell them they can have rice, baked potato, or french fries and their eyes roll back in their head, their mouth opens, and they're gone. They're going to ponder this one for ten minutes? I start to wonder: how do these people make big decisions like what house to buy or what job to take?

Nancy Kelly
New York City

I don't think people understand how a restaurant works. I think they think that the chef makes food for different kinds of people, and they want to know what's good for their kind of person. So they ask, "What should

I have?" It gets complicated, but life is complicated. I say, "You want to hone in a little bit for me? Do you want pasta, vegetables, meat, or fish?" Because as soon as you say, "Oh the pork is really good," they say, "Oh, I don't eat pork." I hate that.

I worked at a four-star restaurant in New York where the food was exceptionally good. He was one of the top chefs on the continent at the time. Mostly people appreciated it, but it was cool to appreciate it, so it's hard to tell if they really appreciated it or not. They would come in with the review and put it down next to them on the table. The four-star review. They would come in, take it out of their purse, unfold it, open the menu, see what they wrote about in the review, and check to see if it was on the menu that week. That's how they would order. And they would be disappointed if what was in the review wasn't on the menu. So it's hard to know if people really liked it or if they just knew that they were supposed to. Especially with a clientele that is that wealthy, because there is such a big facade. They walk in the door with their Chanel outfits and everything, and very rarely will those kind of people show any genuine appreciation.

Freeda Kaufman
Jethro's Bar & Grill
New York City

Pests

I think it is time for a frank discussion about pests. And I don't mean the customers who stop you every time you walk by their table. I'm talking about cockroaches, mice, flies, mosquitoes, and yes, rats.

The fact is, the more we humans try to tame the world around us, the more we realize how unmanageable it actually is. Examples abound: remember that lovely cottage on the beachfront? Good. It's gone. The tide came and swallowed it up. Better look for drier land. How about something in the Hollywood Hills? Too shaky? What about a farm? Maybe a place back where I came from in Oklahoma. It's beautiful there. I would recommend you build your house out of brick though, and don't forget a nice comfortable cellar—the wind can blow awfully hard. It's not so much that nature is encroaching on us, it's more the opposite. And that's where the vermin come in.

I haven't read the latest census figures, but it is my guess that there are more rodents and insects than human beings on earth. We may not see them every day, but rest assured they are around, doing what they like to do most, which is eat. And like we humans, they seem to enjoy a visit to a restaurant. Why not? After all, what is a restaurant but a building full of food? How nice it must be to go out to eat and not have to pay—or tip.

Every restaurant I have ever worked in has had insects and rodents. Every one. Every restaurant you have ever eaten in has had, at one time or another, insects and rodents. Every one. Faithfully the exterminator comes. He sprays, he baits, he traps. Many die, and many more are born to take their place. It is an ongoing battle. Sort of like the one you wage in your home. Still, some restaurants have worse luck than others.

I used to work at a restaurant in New York City with a big rat problem. It seemed like the place was cursed. First of all it was in New York, which, like any large city, has lots of rodents. Secondly, it was near the waterfront, which rats, like humans, seem to find an especially nice place to live. Finally, and perhaps most problematic, it was situated next door to a very dirty deli, which did not use the services of an exterminator. No matter how much we tried to get rid of our rats, there was always a fresh supply living right next door. And the thing about rats is, they can eat through walls. It was spooky. The restaurant had a suspended ceiling; after the guests left and we turned the music down you could hear the rats running back and forth over your head. It sounded like bowling balls rolling down those hardwood lanes. There were incidents. I remember one night when I went up to a customer who was simply ashen. I asked him what the problem was and he said, "A rat!" So I went into my standard disclaimer (this wasn't the first rat sighting, after all) about how this is New York, and there are rats, and we use the best exterminator, and blah, blah, blah. In the middle of my speech he cried out, "IT WAS *ON* ME!" Over the next few minutes I discovered that, in fact, the rat had dropped from a hole in the ceiling onto his shoulder and run down his body to the floor, where it made a dash for the kitchen. I made an executive decision and insisted that we buy his dinner. Having said that, I have no patience for someone who sees a cockroach and wants a free meal. Worse yet, I have heard of customers who see a roach and leave a restaurant. I mean, really. What do they do when they see a roach in their house? Move?

Insects and rodents pretty much do what they want. They don't listen to reason, and they're not bound by social convention. At least not ours. Can you reasonably expect to eat out often and never see a pest? No. If you should see one, just remember two things: don't panic, and, your waiter didn't put it there.

We have a cookie jar in the restaurant where we keep the cookies that we sell. One morning we came in and all the cookies were gone. Everyone was accused of taking them. A few nights later we heard a noise and ran to the front of the restaurant to see a skunk with the lid of the cookie jar in his paws, eating a cookie. That night we started leaving a pie pan out with lettuce in it for the skunk to eat. After that he left the cookies alone. One night we forgot to put the lettuce out and the skunk shit in the pan. We never saw him again.

> Rose Larsen
> Rose's Den at the Boulder Inn
> Milepost 28, Highway 93
> Kingman, Arizona

Anyone who is freaked out about seeing a roach is stupid. This is New York.

> Russell Dean Anderson
> Miracle Grill
> New York City

In New York I worked in a place where you could ride the rats across the kitchen. They were so big you could saddle them. But things like rodents and bugs have never bothered me—we're living in a city and it's part of city living. But I think they bother restaurant customers, and I think that's totally unrealistic. I remember in my restaurant in New York once we had a problem with palmetto bugs, these flying roaches. It was spring and we had all the windows open and one flew in and landed on the wall. One of the customers freaked out, as if this weren't something that would land in her car or on her windowsill. She freaked out like it was the end of the world. And that just amazes me, that someone would react that way in a city. It is a *fact of life.*

Ray Proscia
Georgia
West Hollywood, California

In New York there are always rodents and roaches crawling all over the place. And that's what you say, "It's New York." They're crawling across the table, "It's New York," or, "They sprayed." That's what everyone always says, "We sprayed this week, so they're really out in force now before they die."

Michael Salmons
Braque
New York City

We had a rat run through a four-star restaurant I was working in. There were rats in the basement and we didn't know what to do about it. We had to change down there and they were big. Anyhow, the dining room was a rectangle and the food came out through an opening at one of the ends of the room. Through the opening was the waiters' station and a hallway that led to the kitchen. All of a sudden a rat ran across the opening and back. So this table saw the rat, but being a very white, WASP restaurant, nobody screamed. But the waiter saw it, and the customers who saw it called him over, and he went and got the owner, and she said, "I'm sorry, I'm sorry, I'm sorry, we killed it." But we didn't. We didn't know where it was. We had no idea where it was. So the whole night we spent in total anxiety that it was going to come out again. We had to give them the whole dinner for free, and it was like $600.

Freeda Kaufman
Jethro's Bar & Grill
New York City

They're everywhere. In every kind of restaurant I've ever worked in. Some customers freak out when they see a bug and other's don't at all. I think it depends on whether they have ever waited tables or not. I had this one table of people who saw a roach on the table and immediately stopped dining, had us take all the food away, and walked out of the restaurant. I think they were from New Jersey. They had *pretentions* to Manhattan. So I'm telling you all if you're reading this book, there are bugs in every restaurant you eat in.

Waiter X
Khin Khao
New York City

When you serve fresh produce, and especially organic produce, which hasn't been treated with pesticides, you run the risk of having bugs. I once served a garden salad in New York and one of the leaves leapt off the plate. It was a big green bug. But most people are pretty understanding; they know it's not your fault. I did have these women from Spain the other day who were upset that there were flies in the restaurant. We had the patio doors open so there was really nothing we could do about the flies, but they wanted to move to a different table. So we moved them. Of course there was a fly near their new table also. One of the women was drinking a glass of wine and this fly lands on the lip of the glass. She calls me over and tells me the fly touched the wine. The glass was about half full, so I went and got her a new glass of wine—also about half full. She was incensed that I didn't bring her a full glass of wine. And she tipped me accordingly.

Gregg Ostrin
Beverly Hills, California

I worked in a seafood restaurant where a guy got to the bottom of his salad and there was a roach. The whole party left. They didn't even stay for their entrées, they just left. But there are more bugs in my home than there are in any restaurant. And I think you could say that about the customers' homes, too.

Gary Chiappa
Roettele A.G.
New York City

Most restaurants in New York have a cat to keep the mice and rats at bay. My friend Fred saw a mouse at the restaurant recently. He went running through the kitchen screaming. Of course, the whole staff was making fun of him because he's a man and he's afraid of a mouse. But we don't have any major problems. Lots of roaches, but everywhere there are lots of roaches.

Stacey Jurewicz
Pescatore
New York City

I've never seen a rodent in a restaurant but this one woman found a screw in her salad. She said, "What is this doing here?" and I said, "We felt that you weren't getting enough iron in your diet. We're looking out for your well-being."

Doug V.
Los Angeles, California

I was working in a restaurant in Hell's Kitchen, New York City, about five or six years ago. We were closing up and most of the staff had gone downstairs to count the money. There was one other waitress up-stairs with me and about four customers sitting at two different tables. I went to the bathroom at the back of the restaurant. I know this bathroom like the back of my hand and I have a certain routine; I would walk in the bathroom and with one hand shut the door and lock it, and with the other hand unbutton and unzip my jeans. Then as I walked toward the commode I would have my pants down and turn around to pee all in one motion. For some reason, that night I looked be-hind me. And there, everybody's worst fear, was a rat in the toilet bowl. So I screamed, and ran, and didn't look back, and of course I had locked the door and was pulling my up my pants and I couldn't get out of there fast enough. Everybody in the restaurant heard me. The Mexicans who worked there were all excited and came running in to try to kill the rat but he had al-ready swam back down underwater. I hear that rats can swim for three minutes underwater. I don't know where he came from but he was big and he was as scared as I was, and I have never sat down on a toilet seat in the ground floor of a building again, including homes.

> Cyndi Raftus
> Hourglass Tavern
> New York City

A roach once ran up Martin Sheen's arm as he was ordering and I was unable to say a word. Willem Dafoe, a regular, was eating one night while I was working alone and told me he had just seen a rat. We thought it went into the kitchen but a few minutes later it was barreling down the space behind the counter straight at me; red eyes, and fast as hell. I screamed, and Willem dashed be-hind the counter, pushed me behind him, and stomped it until it was dead. He wiped off his shoe and finished his dinner; I love him.

Cherie Hamblin
Moondance Diner
New York City

At my first job in New York City, I still had a strong southern accent. And you know people from the North have this stereotype about people from down South; that everybody lives out in the country and knows all about animals and critters and stuff. Well, the owner spots a baby mouse in the dining room and it was hiding under tables and running around and everybody was freaking out. For some reason he thought that I would know what to do. So I got a teacup and a cocktail napkin and I got it and walked out and released it on 42nd Street.

Bridget Munger
Arthur's Landing
Weekhawken, New Jersey

The places that I've worked at have been really good at trying to control the pest situation, but it is impossible not to have rodents in New York City—they're all over the place. And that's another funny thing about customers; there have been a couple of times, especially with salads, where a customer has found a tiny green caterpillar on a leaf of lettuce. I mean everything is washed thoroughly. But I get the impression that people would like to have their food put on Ground Zero at Hiroshima and blasted free of any kind of nature. They just can't cope with the fact that they are part of a food chain. They find this tiny green caterpillar and people look at me as if I have just vomited on their plate. And then they want the world given to them. They want me to get down and

kiss their feet and beg their forgiveness. Things do go
wrong. And anyway, if they ate the caterpillar it would
probably have more nutrition that what they've got in
front of them.

Chico Garcia
Midnight Lake
New York City

Holidays

The holiday season is upon me. It is December 13, 1993. When I woke up this morning I immediately started wrestling with my conscience. Should I begin my Christmas shopping, which might make it possible for the gifts to arrive at their distant destinations by Christmas, or start writing this chapter, which might make it possible to meet my deadline? Since it's 30° F. with a stiff north wind outside, I chose to write.

I'm one of those people who is ambivalent about most holidays. I vacillate between liking them and hating them for various reasons. Many people I know are like this. It may have something to do with adulthood; when you are a kid holidays mean long, uninterrupted stretches of time off from school. When you grow up you get a day off for the actual holiday, and maybe an extra day here and there (assuming you don't work for the federal government or New York City, in which case you get all those days *and* every Monday off). That is, unless you are a waiter. Waiters work on holidays. I'm not sure, but this may influence the way I feel about these occasions.

Thanksgiving might be my favorite holiday. The idea that

we gather with friends and loved ones to give thanks for the blessings that have been bestowed upon us is a wonderful one. For me this holiday has several other good features: it is in the autumn, which is my favorite season; it can be interpreted as religious or nonreligious, according to your inclination; and you get to eat a huge amount of food. So far so good. Unfortunately, I had to work this year. And last year. I can't believe the restaurant was even open. I was mortified to see my name on the schedule for Thursday, November 25. I mean, what kind of a loser eats out on Thanksgiving Day? Even if I didn't have a friend in the world, or if I couldn't boil water, I wouldn't go to a restaurant on this holiday. I would rather eat a Swanson TV dinner. And I'm a vegetarian. It is the quintessential stay-at-home day. I don't get it. In fairness I should say that the owners of my restaurant did a couple of things that made the shift tolerable; they didn't give the guests a choice of what they could eat, which makes getting an order out of someone less of a challenge, and they made the price of the meal really high, so that even if somebody left a miserly tip (think about it, there are people who will leave a poor schmuck a lousy tip on Thanksgiving Day) percentage-wise it didn't kill you. But I still resented working.

Most restaurants are closed Christmas Day. Rare is the restaurant owner (that breed of person who would sell their own mother for a buck) who dares to ask the staff to work on this day. Plus, it would probably be slow. But the weeks preceding Christmas are very busy indeed. You get tons of office parties, which are so predictable that they are mind-numbing. At these affairs there is no integration; the management sits at one end of the table (or their own table for that matter), and the peons sit at the other. The management folks always have pained expressions on their faces; you know that they are longing to slip into the leather interior of their car and get away from the underlings. The underlings have their own getaway in mind—they are going to drink themselves unconscious. Things get said. Feelings get hurt. We add the tip.

New Year's Eve is a big night in the restaurant world. The owner of the first restaurant I worked in called New Year's

Eve "amateur night." He said, "Guys come out, drink five rum and Cokes, and go home and beat up their wives." Sadly, I think this is probably an accurate characterization. Since I believe this to be the stupidest holiday of the year, I am glad to work. It's always the same: we do two seatings, we charge a huge amount of money, we include the tip on the check, we watch people make asses of themselves, and we go home with the rent. It is a bit melancholy though, because I always get the impression that people feel they would be having a much better time if they were only somewhere else. But people feel that way no matter where they are on New Year's Eve. I'm not one for telling people what to do, but I'm willing to go out on a limb here. Do you want to have a better time than any of your friends this New Year's Eve? Stay home with a good book.

Next on the calendar is Valentine's Day. Another big restaurant day. Even in this era of ardent feminism, a guy is pretty much duty-bound to take his wife or girlfriend out to eat on February 14. The other option is to spend the day building yourself a doghouse to live in. Why has the holiday evolved to be one where the guy has to shower gifts on the woman? Who knows? I'll work the shift. The only drawback is that you have to wait on a million tables—all of them deuces. On the other hand, sometimes you get to witness a pretty good argument.

Saint Patrick's Day is a drag to work in New York City. Keep the mop handy.

There is one more big restaurant holiday, and it is the biggest one of all. Mother's Day. I don't work Mother's Day. Period. Yes, it is the busiest day of the year for a restaurant. Yes, you can make a lot of money. No, it's not worth it. Too much tension.

Working holidays is a fact of life for most waiters and waitresses. I guess it could be worse; we could work in movie theaters—they're open on Christmas day. I resent working on some holidays, but I am also resigned to doing it as long as I work in the restaurant business. I wondered how other waitpeople felt about it though, so I asked the men and women I interviewed to share their thoughts about holidays with me.

In New York I don't mind it so much, but in Florida I hated it. I love to be with my family on holidays. But I also don't like being alone on holidays, so here I prefer to work. Your coworkers are like a family in most restaurants. I think it's sad that restaurants are open on holidays. I also think that people who come to restaurants on holidays should compensate us for working. Another thing I forget is that Christmas is just a *Christian* holiday. We were packed on Christmas Day. Packed. We made so much money. But we had to wait on the owner and ten of his friends and they didn't leave us anything. Nothing. And the worst part was that they tried to lie about it. They claimed they left us $30 on the table, but they didn't.

Stacey Jurewicz
Pescatore
New York City

Thanksgiving is really sad. People come in by themselves, which makes me feel terrible. It kills me to see people having Thanksgiving dinner alone. And they all act like it's okay. You go to take their order and they're all happy and they say, "Oh, I think I'll have the turkey breast!"

On New Year's Eve you feel better because at least you're making money, but it's hideous. People think it's an excuse to act like a farm animal and it grosses me out. I worked in one restaurant downtown that was very chic, and these people would get on the tables and pull their dresses up over their heads, and it's like, *what* are you doing?

Well, I'm gay. I think Valentine's Day is gross. You turn all the four-tops into two-tops and it's all straight people. But at least people mind their own business more on Valentine's Day, as long as you bring the heart-shaped strawberry tart on time.

I live in New York so I get a big kick out of Mother's Day. Because all these very fabulous people come in with their mothers. And they are *mothers,* there is no way around it. And it's like, of course you're going to get a bad tip, so you just kind of write that off. But it is the busiest day of the year, because everybody has to take their mother out, even though they hate her.

> Waiter X
> Khin Khao
> New York City

Mother's Day is a fucking nightmare. It's the busiest restaurant day of the year. Everybody's mother is so important. So the restaurant is overflowing with customers, and you can't handle them all no matter what you do. It's the worst day for tips. It's a miserable, horrible deal to work. And if you go out it's worse—the food's always bad, it's all pre-prepared. When I get hired I tell the manager that I'll work Thanksgiving but I won't work Mother's Day.

> Gary Chiappa
> Roettele A.G.
> New York City

I don't really like working on the Fourth of July. Everyone is out seeing fireworks so it's not really busy.

> Kelsey Geisler
> Trompe L'oeil
> New York City

I hate working Thanksgiving because it's my favorite holiday. I'd rather just be cooking or at someone's house. I've never worked Christmas Day, and I never would, but I don't mind working Christmas Eve. It's nice and busy leading up to Christmas, but I get such a bad holiday attitude that I can't enjoy it. And it's not just about waiting tables, it's the whole thing.

As far as New Year's Eve goes, I'd rather be in a midnight fire at sea than work it. I just can't stand it. Everyone has this plan to go out and get fucked up, and I can't stand being around people like that. I can't stand Saint Patrick's Day for the same reason. The only difference is that it's green beer that they're throwing up.

Mother's Day is the worst. There is nothing worse than a Mother's Day brunch. It's nothing but unhappy people who would otherwise not be spending the day with their mothers. That's what bugs me about the day whether I'm working or not; that it takes some sort of Hallmark idea for these people to acknowledge their mothers.

> Geoff N.
> New York City

Working holidays generally sucks. Because when you come to a restaurant on Thanksgiving or Christmas it is the second-best option. Or the third-best option. And usually what is going to happen is a drunken debauch. And it's going to be *my* fault that they're in a restaurant instead of being with their family or their friends. But they'll tell themselves, "This is exactly what I wanted to do; I wanted to sit here and get drunk on Christmas Eve." It's like a payday Friday, full moon drunk. I hate it, it's depressing.

The only holiday that is worth working is New Year's Eve. Instead of chasing around town trying to find something more exciting, the party comes to you. And you get paid for it. It's the ultimate way to spend New Year's Eve because there are no gaps in the conversation at a boring party, and you're not worried about what is going on somewhere else. The same is true about Halloween, which is another trumped-up excuse for a holiday.

Valentine's Day is just one party of two after another. You can't get any orders because they're just staring into each other's eyes. And once again they're coming to a restaurant for something we can't really do: they're coming to experience a romantic feeling. I think it is really their own responsibility to provide that. All we can do is put those little conversation hearts on the plates.

Mark Collins
Universal Grill
New York City

Disasters

My least favorite lesson of adulthood is that bad things happen all the time. They happen to good people and they happen at inopportune moments. I resist this notion at every turn, ever hopeful when life is going well that it will somehow stay that way. And then I go to work.

The Random House Dictionary defines a disaster as "a calamitous event, especially one causing great damage or hardship."[2] While this describes the very nature of work for some people, a disaster, of varying degrees, is what you may face in a restaurant on any given night. Restaurant disasters can take many different forms; when you realize, for instance, at nine o'clock on a Saturday night with the restaurant full and an hour wait, that you have run out of champagne glasses and you don't have enough for everyone at the table where you have just sold two bottles of $120-a-bottle champagne, you have one kind of disaster on your hands. If someone be-

[2]*The Random House Dictionary,* concise ed. (New York: Random House, 1980) 249

comes seriously ill in the restaurant you have a different kind altogether. Within the scope of these two disasters lies a world of hardship for a waiter.

Recently I experienced what I would consider a disaster at work. I was the late waiter, so my shift started at seven o'clock. I got to the restaurant comfortably early and went down the front stairs to change into my uniform. As I ascended the back staircase, a treacherous ladderlike affair that connects the kitchen to the basement, I noticed that water was cascading down the stairs. As I got to the top I saw a plumber feverishly working at the hot water heater. It seems our hot water heater had chosen to go out on Friday night. The plumber had somehow managed to locate a new one though, and it was standing in a huge box right in front of the pickup window. For the next two hours we had to navigate through a kitchen with an inch of standing water on the floor and go around the line to pick up our food from the chef's side. Finally, at nine o'clock they opened the box and installed the new water heater, only to find that a part was missing and that we wouldn't have hot water until the next day anyhow. This was an incredible hardship for the waitstaff, since we had to dry each piece of cutlery (which had been washed in cold water) by hand, and practically swim through the kitchen all night. It was a real disaster for the guests, however, as cold water doesn't kill many germs. Suffice to say, the staff wasn't eating or drinking at work that night. Of course, short of nuclear warfare, there is no disaster that could make a restaurant owner close on a Friday night. That would cost money.

Another disaster that comes to mind is a choking incident that happened at the first restaurant I ever worked in. I was sixteen years old and working at a steak house called The Ancestor Restaurant in Stillwater, Oklahoma. It was a very busy night, and in the middle of the chaos a woman at one of my tables began to exhibit all the classic signs of choking: her hands were at her neck and she was unable to speak or breathe. We immediately dialed 911 and EMS arrived almost instantly. Fortunately for all involved, they were located about a block from the restaurant. When the paramedics arrived she was losing consciousness. By this time the entire restaurant had come to a standstill and there was a great deal of tension in the air. One of the paramedics lifted her from the chair and started performing the Heimlich Maneuver. Wrapping his arms under her rib cage he squeezed her with tremendous force. He did this three times with no results, and her skin was beginning to take on a strange pallor. The fourth time he jerked her so hard that her head whipped back and smacked into his, raising an egg-sized lump on his forehead. But her throat was cleared, and the blockage, a one- by four-inch piece of steak, was ejected from her mouth. Her husband thanked the paramedics and after a few minutes began helping his wife toward the door. Everyone was immensely relieved. From the owner's point of view the real disaster was averted when he stopped the man on the way out and told him that in spite of what had happened he was still responsible for his check.

Another disaster that can happen in a restaurant is a robbery or a theft. As the fabric of our society unravels, it seems that this sort of thing has become quite commonplace. In New York, restaurants don't even bother to call the police when they're robbed unless someone is hurt. The police probably wouldn't come anyway.

The ways that a restaurant can be victimized are many. Robbers generally come in at the end of the night with a weapon and simply demand the contents of the cash register. Theives sometimes come in the daytime disguised as inspectors (health department, fire system, etc.), poke around until they're not being watched, and take anything of value they can find. They also strike when the restaurant is really busy and pick people's pockets, or steal women's purses that are on the floor. But the most grievous example of this type of crime is the theft of the tip cup.

In restaurants where waiters pool tips, all the tips from all the tables are put into a tip cup (a coffee can or some similar vessel) and divided equally, or according to a point system, at the end of the night. The tip cup is usually kept behind the bar, out of reach of the guests and any ne'er-do-wells. But twice in my career as a waiter, in two different restaurants, the tip cup has been stolen. Each time this happened the restaurant was uncontrollably busy. In some restaurants there are times when the room is so full of people, and it is so loud, and there is so much going on, that anything can happen. On this kind of night there is no way to restrain the guests; the staff is simply outnumbered. As order breaks down, the guests begin to stand in the service area of the bar, where the waiters pick up their drinks. This adds immeasurably to the confusion of a busy night. You are forced to call your drink orders out to the bartender (who is already swamped) over these interlopers' heads, and push through them to pick up the drinks (when and if they ever get made). On two occasions in the middle of this kind of pandemonium I have looked up and seen the tip cup gone. There were bitter accusations. Why wasn't the host paying attention? How did somebody get behind the bar? Why didn't the bartender keep his customers in line? The waiters were inconsolable. The only thing certain was that after a long, hard night, we were going home with no money. A disaster.

I wanted to find out what kinds of bad or unusual things had happened while other people were waiting tables, so I asked waiters and waitresses to tell me if they had ever witnessed a disaster in a restaurant.

I worked at this private club called the Regency Club in Los Angeles. It was all oil money. It was sickening. And one Christmas Eve I had to work. I was waiting on a party of four and they were just awful. They made me stand outside the door of the room—they didn't want me around. We had these big silver coffeepots and I was refilling coffee when the handle came loose from the pot, showering the table. I was so happy.

At Orso some guy had a heart attack. So the EMS guys come and they put him on a stretcher, and the room is all quiet and looking at him. On the way out he lifts up his head and yells, "IT WASN'T THE FOOD!"

Bob Dombroski
Orso
New York City

I used to manage this Italian trattoria in Sydney. I would walk in there in the morning and the chef would be there after a night on smack and he'd be standing, asleep on his feet, chopping up vegetables with his eyes closed. I'd walk in there at ten o'clock and he'd be on the nod. What do you say? "Hey, Giles, why don't you put that down for a second and we'll go out and have a cappuccino together?" I sat in the back of a cab once, with a glass full of ice with his thumb in the bottom, on the way to the hospital to see if they could reattach it. That was a disaster.

Chico Garcia
Midnight Lake
New York City

I worked on MacDougal Street and a man living in the building opposite my restaurant took some of his family hostage and started shooting into the street at policemen who had answered his wife's call. Because it was such a loud, busy street, we had no idea that any of this was happening until our front window exploded and the SWAT team ran in screaming for everyone to get down. We all hid in the kitchen, customers, too, for hours. They blocked off the street and were waiting the guy out. My manager was making the police really mad by swinging the door open in a panic every ten minutes or so, asking when we could come out. I forget what time it started, but I remember going home at 2:00 A.M.; we usually closed at midnight. We all ate happily in the kitchen, and the customers almost had to pay because the manager was so freaked out. They put up a fight and walked out laughing—there were only two or three couples. They ended up shooting the sniper, as we were fond of calling him.

At Moondance once there was a big storm and the restaurant was hit by lightning. Since the diner is a big metal pie tin it became electrified. We called the fire department after the lights went out and they told us not to touch anything. They were asking us if we had rubber-soled shoes on, and where the door was in relation to the telephone. The front was made of heavy metal so they were concerned about how we were going to get out because the restaurant might have exploded. We had to stand in the middle of the diner as if we had bees on us until they came.

> Cherie Hamblin
> Moondance Diner
> New York City

At my very first waiting job, on my very first day, I spilled a glass of water all over a man and he jumped up and said, "I've been baptized!" I was humiliated.

> Maryanne Contreras
> Los Angeles, California

I had a manager who stole all the money from the restaurant to go to Las Vegas on a cocaine binge. He also stole money from me. I was going to deposit the cash for my rent that night but he took all the money out of my wallet. I was very upset. The guy left his wife and child, and took all the money from the weekend receipts—which must have been around $10,000. They caught him because he rented a car with his credit card, and gave his real address and telephone number. He kept the car longer than he said he was going to and when they called his wife she asked where he was and they told her he was in Las Vegas.

> Doug V.
> Los Angeles, California

I've witnessed somebody's purse getting stolen; I've witnessed too many fights to remember. A lot of fights. Somebody was murdered right outside last week. Rose-land is across the street and last week this gang of kids chased another kid out of that club and beat the shit out of him right out front. He died. And I felt so helpless. There's nothing you can do. I'm a waitress; I can't run outside and say, "Okay, guys, cut it out." And one of the waitresses wanted to go take pictures with her camera. I said, "What are you doing? This isn't *People* magazine, this is real life." But aside from that I think disasters and emergencies are kind of exciting. Even when somebody's purse gets stolen and she's hysterical there is part of me that just wants to laugh. You know? It's a sick reaction. There's a mean streak that comes across you when you're waiting tables and somebody's purse gets stolen. I just say, "Oh, let me get the manager."

Shawna Mason
Lone Star Roadhouse
New York City

I saw probably the worst thing you would ever want to see in a restaurant. At Legal Seafood we were in the bottom of a hotel and we had notoriously bad ventilation. People would come in and eat a bowl of clam chowder, a three-pound lobster, and a big ice cream sundae, and they'd be sitting there and they'd realize how much cholesterol they had just ingested—the gout is already starting to set in—and they'd just pass out, or throw up. You'd see people sprinting to the bathroom with bibs on, and a lot of them didn't make it. Some of them would just slump in their chairs. You know, they've had fourteen drinks waiting three hours for their table, then they put down a three-pound lobster and they're sick. But the guy I'm thinking of had a heart attack. There was a little platform that looked out over the restaurant, and my wife was working that station. This was before we even started dating. So this guy went down in her station. It was all deuces and one big round table in the station. This guy went down and he's lying there. They stretch him out, clear a little space for him, and they're patting him down with wet towels. But basically everybody was just waiting around for the ambulance to come. It's a real tense situation and everything has sort of stopped in this area waiting for this guy. He's sort of conscious, but he's obviously not well at all. So Paula was up there just making sure all her tables knew everything was okay, that the ambulance was coming. In the middle of all this, a customer waves his hand for her to come over to the table. She thought he was going to ask if the guy on the floor was all right, or tell her he was a doctor or something. She goes over to the table and the guy says, "Is our food coming any time soon, or what? What's going on back there in the kitchen?" That was sickening. We had a little more leeway there than you do on the West Coast, so she told the guy, "You're unbelievable, pal."

Garrett Harker
San Francisco, California

We have a dish called Pescatore for Two, which is seafood baked over pasta. It has several different kinds of seafood, including lobster, which is in the shell. Recently I was waiting on a man and his date, and he ordered that dish. I guess he cut his thumb on the shell, and it started bleeding profusely. The blood was gushing out all over his hand. Then it formed a puddle on the table about five inches around. He just kept eating, as did his dinner companion. At one point he put his thumb in his water glass, and the water turned beet red. Finally we gave him a napkin to wrap his hand in. He never went to the rest room the entire time. As he was leaving he said, "Maybe I should sue you guys," and I said, "Maybe we should sue *you* for offending us." It was disgusting.

Stacey Jurewicz
Pescatore
New York City

I was up in the Catskills and I got a job in a Holiday Inn. It was a Polynesian restaurant, so you can imagine how cheesy it was, right? I had this party of thirteen women and the whole table was covered with a pupu platter. The pupu platter was being heated from below; not by sterno cans, but by that blue glop that they put in a bowl. For some reason it exploded. It just exploded. There was soot and black everywhere. When the smoke cleared they were just black. And *wailing*. They were very unhappy. We cleaned them up as best as we could and they went back to their rooms and changed. The manager took their clothes and had them dry cleaned. It was a disaster.

Gary Chiappa
Roettele A.G.
New York City

In my restaurant we have these booths against the wall that are very deep. When the customers sit in one of these booths they are hard to see, and somewhat hard to serve. Anyway, I was waiting on these two couples in one of the booths, and they were restaurateurs from Palos Verdes. They were drinking up a storm. One of the women was so drunk that she got really sick and started throwing up at the table. She's coughing up her guts. We got all these cloth napkins and covered up the vomit on the table, and then I was needed at another table. Well, my boss, who is in his Armani suit and who hasn't bussed a table in twenty years, comes by and sees all these napkins on the table. Well, these are such very special customers that he says, "Oh, let me take those napkins for you!" unaware of what was within. It wasn't until he got to the linen bin that he realized that he was holding two handfuls of vomit. That's the best disaster I've ever witnessed.

Gregg Ostrin
Beverly Hills, California

I've never seen anything really bad. I guess I have an angel looking over my shoulder. I did see one thing that was sort of a disaster, though. It was in a restaurant where we didn't use trays; we stacked plates along our arms to take them out. And this is sort of a pet peeve, too. Without fail you would be walking by a table with ten plates on each arm and a customer would stop you and ask you for something. Anyway, I was working with this girl who was about to quit her job, and she was walking by this table with about a hundred plates on her arms and they asked her for some ketchup. She looked at them and said, "Sure, let me get that for you," dropped all the plates on the floor at their feet, went and got a bottle of ketchup and said, "Can I bring you anything else at the moment?"

Waiter X
Khin Khao
New York City

When I was seventeen I worked at this place called Farrell's Ice Cream Parlor. They were all over California and they were known as *the* place to go for your birthday. We had these big things known as the zoo; it was this big silver bowl about the size of a punch bowl and it had all these different flavors of ice cream in it. This thing fit in a stretcher, and you'd put the stretcher over your shoulders and they'd ring this bell and someone would scream, "LADIES AND GENTLEMEN, HAVING A BIRTHDAY!" and you'd run through the restaurant and out into the street and back into the restaurant and to the table with this thing. We were right down the street from a high school, so on Friday nights the football teams and all the kids would come in. So one night we were running this thing through the restaurant and one of the football players tripped me. The whole thing went flying and I fell down on the floor. It was really embarrassing. But that whole restaurant was embarrassing. It was embarrassing to work there, the outfit you had to wear was embarrassing, and doing this birthday schtick was embarrassing. Because there was a birthday every five minutes. And that was the point, really. I mean, little kids came in and loved it, but adults would bring their friends there just to embarrass them.

I remember one night these four women came in and

one of them was really prim and proper, and it was her birthday. So we brought the stretcher out, and in addition to all the other stuff when we served it, we would pull their chair by its back and scream, "JUMPING TO HER FEET WITH EXCITEMENT!" So I pulled her chair and screamed the line, and I guess she had no reflexes, because she just dropped to the floor. She was really mad. And the madder she got the harder I laughed. Some people got really bent out of shape.

Holly Gagnier
Los Angeles, California

We had a party for this famous composer at a four-star restaurant where I worked. Vladimir Horowitz was there, Leonard Bernstein, Louise Nevelson; it was star-studded. Telegrams were coming in from all over the world during the meal. Jessye Norman was there; it was in the old place, and it's a small room. You knew everybody who was there. It was his ninetieth birthday, and it was this fabulous birthday party for him. Everything had to be done just so. We had a piano brought in, there were opera singers, everything was right up there. So they made a huge cake with ninety of those really tall, elegant candles on it. They put it on a marble slab, lit the candles, and one of the waiters came out of the kitchen with it. It was all organized—the lights dimmed, the candles were lit, he came out with the cake, a waiter is walking in front of him with a menu shielding the candles so they wouldn't blow out, and everybody starts to sing. The opera singers are singing happy birthday . . . it sounds amazing . . . and just as he gets close to the guest of honor, the cake starts to slide. It just slides, and slides, and slides until it hits the floor. The waiter died. He was so embarrassed. And the worst part was the opera singers just trailed off—Happy Birth . . . day . . . dear . . . And *silence*. The cake was a giant chocolate mousse cake and it had just folded into itself on the floor. Ninety candles were sticking every which way out of the pile. We had to turn the lights up and scrape the thing off of the floor. The magic was lost. It was unbelievable. And the owner got up and said, "Our staff is the best in the world, but sometimes accidents happen." You couldn't talk to the waiter about it for weeks. He's never forgiven himself for it.

Freeda Kaufman
Jethro's Bar & Grill
New York City

I worked at this continental restaurant in Gainesville, Florida. It was Steak Diane tableside, Caesar salad tableside, and a variety of flambé desserts all done at tableside. The waiters at this place started playing jokes on one another; you know how you get bored in a restaurant and you start fooling around. I was waiting on some of my regular customers and they had ordered some kind of flambé dessert—Bananas Foster, or Peach Flambé or something. When you make these desserts you flame it with rum, and we were using 85 proof. I got the pan really hot, because the hotter you get the pan the higher the flames leap up. I put a little rum in the pan and it practically exploded. There was this fireball that singed all the hair off of my arm and almost lit up this lady's hairdo. I dropped the pan on the floor. I had to. All of a sudden the carpet is on fire and I'm trying to stamp it out and my shoes start to burn. The owner, K.J., came running over with this big pitcher of water and doused my feet and the carpet. The fire was out, but now I'm soaked. It's about 8:30 and I'm going to have to walk around with soggy feet for the rest of the night. I looked around the corner and the other waiters are like Larry, Moe, and Curly, they're just dying laughing. It turns out they had switched 151-proof rum with the 85. It blew up on me! It could have burned the lady's head off. But the worst part was that the other tables in my section were going, "Do it again! We want that dessert!"

Matt Jaroszewicz
Gainesville, Florida

At a restaurant where I worked in New York the kitchen got too hot one night and the fire system deployed. It sprayed white foam all over everything, including the food. It was amazing though, they had the whole thing up and running in forty-five minutes. Another time, at the same restaurant, Immigration came and the entire kitchen staff had to leave.

The big disaster for us here is if the computer goes down. Because it does everything; it sends your drink orders to the bar, your food orders to the kitchen, and it totals your checks. I don't even know any of the prices on the menu. So when it goes down it's over. Also, in Los Angeles you have earthquakes to worry about. But they almost never happen during service; they seem to always happen early in the morning. Then of course there were the riots. When that happened we got everybody out pretty quickly. They didn't even have to pay, we just said, "Leave."

When I first got the job at The Grill I served Burt Lancaster his food and there was broccoli on the plate. I thought he was going to have a heart attack about that. That was a *real* disaster. You haven't lived until you've had Burt Lancaster screaming at you about broccoli on his plate. He said, "Broccoli is for PIGS! *Never* serve a person broccoli!"

Michael K.
The Grill
Beverly Hills, California

Once I had a huge tray of drinks and somebody bumped me and I dropped the whole thing. Well, this glass of red wine spilled all over this lady. Fortunately she was wearing black. I mean, you can imagine how terrible it would have been if she were wearing white. And she was really kind of okay about it, but I was incredibly upset. When I went back to the bar the bartender said, "Here," and gave me this big shot of tequila, which I promptly drank. Then I thought, *"What am I doing?* Now I'm going to go spill again."

Kelsey Geisler
Trompe L'oeil
New York City

Once in my restaurant in New York there was an electrical problem in the coatroom and it went up in flames. It was a Friday night and the place was packed. The whole place started filling up with smoke and the customers wouldn't leave. The firemen came and were knocking the wall down, and they didn't care. They just sat there eating. It was ridiculous.

Ray Proscia
Georgia
West Hollywood, California

I accidentally knocked an old lady across the room once and three male customers had to pick her up. It was hell.

Robin Maynor
Linn's Fruit Bin
Cambria, California

The first month we were open there were three heart attacks and two strokes. I swear to God. Fortunately, the paramedics are right behind the restaurant. We were going to get a direct line. It was amazing, people dropping right and left. It was like, hello, is it the food? It got to where we thought we were going to have to start checking people's pulse rate on the way in, because we didn't need the bad publicity. It's the worst thing in the world when you're waiting on a table and all of a sudden the woman is *in* her lobster bisque.

Robin Shipley
Granita
Malibu, California

We are in the middle of seventy miles of desert. At 7:30 one morning a man came running in asking us to call an ambulance. His mother was having a heart attack. We put her on a couch in the bar and I worked on her. We called the closest town, which is twenty miles away. The ambulance was there in twenty minutes, about the same time that the Flight for Life helicopter arrived. They flew her to Las Vegas. The son came back later to thank us; he said she would have been dead in another twenty minutes.

Rose Larsen
Rose's Den at the Boulder Inn
Milepost 28, Highway 93
Kingman, Arizona

I've had a woman set her hair on fire. I told her to be careful of the candle; she ignored me, and the next thing I knew her whole head was on fire. You could smell it all over the restaurant. I told my other customers, "This is Perretti's beauty salon, I'm sorry for the hair burning."

One time at the Warwick Hotel I was waiting on the manager's family. Their food came up and I was carrying it to the table on one of those big trays. Six lobsters, with ramekins full of melted butter and sauce. As I got near the table I felt the tray becoming unbalanced; it was moving slightly forward, and it was going to fall onto the table and all over the manager's family. I had no choice but go for the wall. So this is what the manager saw me do: I took his family's meal and smashed it into the wall. I lasted another week there.

I had a choking once in my restaurant. A man choking on a fish bone. The nurse got it out. I was waiting on a table and the man came late, so I had been chatting with the woman. She told me she was a nurse. At another table I had these three uptight Upper East Siders. They were these two divorcées and their designer friend, who was gay but they were never going to say it. You know the types. Everything had to be just so. He was eating bouillibaisse, and he started to choke. They called me over and said, "Our friend seems to have something lodged in his throat, could you bring us some bread?" I gave him some bread, and the thing was still lodged in his throat . . . along with the bread. Of course, I'm over on the telephone talking to my friend because I'm so bored. They called me back to the table and said, "The bread didn't seem to work. Do you know the Heimlich Maneuver?" I said, "No, but I've got a nurse right over here." I went over to her table and said, "Excuse me, there's a man over there choking; could you come over and have a look at him?" She said sure, finished her soup, and went over to his table. I went back to the telephone. She did the Heimlich, the fish bone came up, he dabbed his mouth with his napkin, and finished his meal. It was very elegant.

> Ted LoRusso
> Perretti's
> New York City

I dropped a tray with a well done T-bone on it once. And it takes twenty minutes to cook one. This was at Sam's Town in Vegas. Of course the customer was pissed off at me. It was an accident; it happens.

> Becky Milici
> Fama
> Santa Monica, California

When I worked at Benny's Burrito's it was always busy and very crowded. We also carried our own banks in bags at our waist. One night this woman was sitting by herself, waiting for a friend, and she had her dry cleaning with her. Her friend shows up and she gets up to greet him and they kind of sandwich me between them. The dry cleaning is in there, and in the confusion she takes my bag, with about $700 in it, and shoots down Avenue A. I ran out the door after her but I lost her in Tompkin's Square Park. I called a police car over and I got in the back seat. So we're driving through the park looking for her and they get a call over the radio that a car that people had been selling firearms out of had been spotted nearby. All of a sudden they stop looking for my robber and start chasing this Cadillac. I said, "Guys, I've gotta go back to work," and they said, "We can't let you go right now." The next thing I know we're going over the Brooklyn Bridge and then we're clear out in Brooklyn. They pull this guy over, and I say, *"Wait,* you guys want to throw me a gun?" These guys had been selling firearms, and I'm thinking they're going to open fire on the cops. They arrest the guys, and by this time I've been gone from Benny's for at least forty-five minutes. On the way back over the bridge the cops are like, "So what's the food like there?" and I'm saying, "Guys, can we hurry? I've got to get back to work." I walk through the front door and the manager says, "Where the hell were you?" and I just said, "Brooklyn."

Did you hear what happened at Boca Chica? Last year, it was in the middle of winter, I think. The busboy opened the door to take out the trash at the end of the night and five guys with sawed-off shotguns forced their way in. They made the waitstaff take their clothes off— all their clothes off, everything—get on their knees in a single-file line, crawl downstairs to the safe, pick it up, and carry it upstairs and put it in their van. Then they drove off with the safe with something like five grand in it. Not only did they rob them, but they *humiliated* them. Could you imagine coming to work the next day? Looking one another in the face? Especially after working eight hours and sweating your ass off, and you're not smelling so good. If you were interested in anybody you worked with that would be out the window.

> Russell Dean Anderson
> Miracle Grill
> New York City

I had a guy throw up all over his girlfriend, but that's about it. Nothing really disastrous like a death or anything. But I think it was a disaster for her. She freaked out, threw her plate, and ran out of the restaurant. He came up and paid the bill with puke all over him and said he was sorry. He was pretty wasted.

Ryan Delmar
Del's Pizzeria
Pismo Beach, California

The most recent disaster we had was a flood. When we had the big rains here Melrose Avenue flooded over. I looked out the window and the water had risen to the sidewalk level, so there was about two feet of water in the street. I went to the manager and said, "The water is rising," and he looked at me and said, "Well, what do you want me to do about it?" I said, "Nothing, I just thought you might want to be aware that it's on the sidewalk now." About fifteen minutes later it came into the restaurant. People, I'm not lying, put their feet up on the chairs and just hung out and drank their beers. Pretty soon it came all the way back to the kitchen. The whole dining room had about a foot and a half of water in it. Finally we had to turn to people and say, "You know what? We're closing up."

Tom Andonian
Los Angeles, California

Health and Safety

Waiters and waitresses face all kinds of hazards at work. Since we come in contact with so many items that other people touch and drink from, we are exposed to every cold and flu that comes through town. We frequently slip and fall on slippery kitchen floors. We cut our hands on knives. We injure our backs carrying heavy trays and lifting things at odd angles. People come into restaurants with guns, rob the restaurant and shoot the waiters. It's a dangerous job. I personally think that smokers pose the greatest threat to waiters' lives. According to an article that appeared in the *Journal of the American Medical Association*, "Waiters and bartenders breathe up to six times more second-hand tobacco smoke than office employees and are one and a half times more likely to develop lung cancer than the public."[3] I asked other waiters and waitresses if they were concerned about their health and safety at work, and what they think about smoking in restaurants. Here is what they told me.

[3](AP) "Smoky Restaurants Pose Risk to Waiters," *New York Newsday* 28 July 1993

I've seen people chop themselves into pieces and scald themselves at the cappuccino machine. Plus, if you're sick and you can't get someone to cover your shift you have to work. When you have the flu you die. You never get better. It's so exhausting, and so smoky. And that's another thing I hate, when people are sitting in the no-smoking section at the end of the night and they say, "Since there's nobody else here can we smoke a cigarette?" And I have to say, "No. It's the no-smoking section," and they say, "But there's nobody else here," and I have to say, "I'm here." People don't think that you have a right to have an opinion or a life if you're a waiter. I work in the no-smoking section because *I don't like smoke*. It doesn't even cross people's minds. And even when you explain it to them they still don't get it. They get indignant.

Waiter X
Khin Khao .
New York City

The Lone Star is a very stressful place to work. It's very crowded, and you get pushed and touched all the time. Sometimes it seems unsafe. For instance, I got into a fight a few weeks ago. An actual, physical fight. There was this group of people there from New Jersey and they drank all night and then refused to pay their check. They said they hadn't drank any of what was on the check. I got the manager and he said it was out of his hands. We have a really bad manager. I told him I wasn't going to go after the money if he wasn't either. Just when I was about to give up this girl said, "I'm not going to pay this check, you @#*%!" She called me this name that I won't repeat. Then she said it again. I lost it. I hit her. And that's not like me. But I hit her. And then she hit me back. Then her boyfriend ran over and held my arms back and I just kept trying to hit her. I think if he hadn't stopped me I would have hit her until I couldn't hit her anymore. When I went home I just felt dirty. You know what I mean? And then I thought about it and I realized that it wasn't her—I can't even remember what she looked like. I was just so angry. Then I got really sad. I was hurt that she called me that name.

Shawna Mason
Lone Star Roadhouse
New York City

I would rather they ban smoking in restaurants because it bugs me. I hate it. I hate working in the smoking section, and especially if I have a cold or something. So I'd be glad if they said you can't smoke in restaurants.

Dickie Mallison
MacArthur Park
San Francisco, California

People just go crazy if they're sat in the smoking section. Half the restaurant is smoking and half the restaurant is nonsmoking, and the nonsmoking fills up first. People will call and the nonsmoking will be booked up, so we'll make a note and tell them that if something opens up in nonsmoking we will move them. But nothing ever opens up, and there is usually only one table smoking anyway; the rest will be people who wanted nonsmoking who don't smoke. And these people come in and say, "But you told us we would be in the nonsmoking section," and they'll bitch and moan and say they have emphysema, or cancer, and some of them will leave. And I just wonder what they did five years ago when there was no nonsmoking section and you just got what you got and you sat there. It's just life or death in the nonsmoking section.

Bob Dombroski
Orso
New York City

I think that the stress of waiting tables is the most dangerous thing about working in a restaurant. It is unlikely that you are going to get burned, unless you are making cappuccino. Oh, there's smoking. I smoke, and I think my job makes me smoke more, so that will probably kill me.

Ted LoRusso
Perretti's
New York City

I smoke, and I think banning smoking in restaurants is a good idea. I hate working in the smoking section. By the end of the night you feel like you have smoked a pack of cigarettes and it ruins you for the rest of the night when you want to go smoke; it's like I've already had my pack.

Doug V.
Los Angeles, California

I smoke a lot, and Moondance allows us to smoke, grudgingly. Since it's too small to be required by New York State law, we have no nonsmoking area and it is amusing when people ask to move away from smokers, their lips pursed in disgust. I happen to feel that smokers have been attacked too violently for their habit, especially in the past few years. I am drawn by the recent ethical dilemmas that have reached restaurants, especially the story about the waiters out West who refused to serve that pregnant woman alcohol. If we serve them the dish we think is disgusting, or the bagel that dropped on the floor when we didn't have time to toast a new one, then I don't think we can begrudge them their own so-called bad choices.

Cherie Hamblin
Moondance Diner
New York City

My biggest concern with health and waiting tables was alcohol. At my old job we'd lock the door at 4:00 A.M., but often we wouldn't leave until the sun came up. But I don't drink anymore. I used to wake up in the morning sometimes and just know that I would probably be dead soon from alcohol.

Gary Chiappa
Roettele A.G.
New York City

I think it's silly to ban smoking from restaurants. I mean, people smoke, and banning smoking from restaurants isn't going to make them smoke any less. We're an addictive culture; we've got to have something in our faces, whether it's alcohol, tobacco, or sugar. The only thing about smoking that I think is really disgusting is when people are eating at a table and one person finishes and lights up a cigarette. I want to take the back of their head and push it into their plate. That, to me, is the rudest, most disgusting thing.

Gregg Ostrin
Beverly Hills, California

Right now my big complaint is smoking. I don't smoke at all, and the place where I work has really low ceilings and poor ventilation. I'm thinking of quitting this job because of it. The smoke coats my throat—it's disgusting. I whine to everybody, and they're sick of hearing it. I'm sorry, but it's disgusting.

Stacey Jurewicz
Pescatore
New York City

I was waiting on tables during the riots. My roommate and I live in West Hollywood, which was in the middle of the riots, and we both work at Granita, which is in Malibu. The city had imposed a curfew, nobody was supposed to be on the streets. Of course every restaurant in the city was closed except ours. We got letters from Wolfgang Puck giving us permission to drive to work. And the police accepted it because Wolfgang is such a big deal in Los Angeles. So we drove in my roommate's pickup truck to work. We're driving past buildings that are on fire, and nobody is out except for the people who are setting the fires and looting. Our pastry chef is this very strong woman, and she told the restaurant that she wasn't coming in until the riots were over because it was too dangerous. She made a stand, everybody else was kissing butt. So I'm waiting on Shirley MacLaine and it comes time for dessert, and she says, "Where's my crème brûlée? I want a crème brûlée." So I tell her we don't have crème brûlée because the pastry department didn't think it was safe to come to work. I explained the situation pretty thoroughly. And she goes, "What are you talking about? What riots? What do you mean? Oh please, it's not that big of a deal." I was amazed. And on the way home we got *shot* at. I risked my life to serve pizza to rich people.

Robin Shipley
Granita
Malibu, California

Owners and Managers

I once worked for a man who put a note on the bulletin board that said we were not allowed to talk to him unless he asked us a question. It was against the rules to say hello to him when he came through the door. This was actually a good thing because he could be quite unpleasant. And it didn't surprise the staff much, because from the start we had been told that he did not accept telephone calls. At all. It didn't matter if it was a wine salesman or a woman claiming to be his mother, we were not to summon him to the telephone. I wouldn't even take a message; I told people straight out that he didn't take calls, that he would call them if he wanted to speak to them. He also loved to drink and carry on. One night he got really shitty and was throwing glasses at me and another waiter. We dodged the projectiles and they exploded against the wall behind us, littering the floor with broken glass. To make amends, he crawled around in the shrapnel. This man owned two restaurants and was quite a successful businessman. Unfortunately, he didn't seem to enjoy it much; he was always depressed, frequently drunk, and terribly jealous of Joe Allen, another successful restaurant owner in midtown Manhattan.

At my first restaurant job, the owner was a hard man. He had worked his way up in the business from the bottom, and he ran a tight ship. I witnessed him fire a waiter for being three minutes late, and a dishwasher for leaning up against a sink. He was tough, but fair in his own way. You knew what the rules were, and that you would lose your job immediately if you broke one of them. I was at an employee meeting once when he told us that he could fire the entire staff on the spot and still open the restaurant that night. A real morale boost. But I, for one, believed him. I think this guy is personally responsible for some of my best work habits—I'm never late for a shift, for instance. But he also loved a drink, as did his wife. There was more than one night when the busboys were dispatched to carry his wife, who was passed out cold, from the bar to the Lincoln. And then the fun would begin. On one such night he brought a busty female customer into the kitchen and unexpectedly pulled her shirt up over her breasts. She slapped him quite hard and ran from the restaurant. He turned to us and said, "I just had to get a look at them."

Until I started working at my current job I believed that all restaurant owners were insane. Now I believe that all but two are. Of course, Richard and Michael used to be waiters, so on one level they don't count. It's like the chicken and the egg; does running a restaurant make you crazy (I know that working in one does), or do crazy people gravitate toward restaurant management and ownership? I don't know if there is an answer to that question—at least not in the pages of this book.

In fairness I would have to say that my experiences with restaurant owners and managers have been mixed. Even the most difficult ones had nice qualities. As I mentioned, my good work habits were instilled in me at my first restaurant job. And in New York, the biggest jerks I have worked for have had a grudging understanding that most of the waitstaff had other interests and tried to be accommodating when it was in their interest to do so.

The relationship between management and the waitstaff is an unusual one to begin with. Waiters usually don't feel all that much allegiance to a restaurant or its owners—they don't pay our salary. And by the same token, restaurant management is armed primarily with a stick, they have but one carrot to offer. A waiter in most restaurants is never going to get a raise or a promotion, as most waiters feel that the manager's job is a step down. The only bargaining chip is the schedule, which restaurant management can use as a double-edged sword, giving you bad shifts as punishment and good ones as reward. This, of course, can affect your income in a dramatic fashion.

I truly like the people I work for now. They listen to the waitstaff and try to strike a genuine balance between our needs and theirs. They are the kind of guys you want to hang out with away from work—smart, funny, and interested in all manner of things. I'm sure I'll remain friends with them long after I quit working at Jethro's Bar & Grill. And one day soon I will quit working there. Some other opportunity will present itself. Waiters are nomads, we move from one job to the next. Maybe that's why most restaurant owners are so insane—just when they get used to one group of people they start moving on. It must break their hearts.

I asked waiters and waitresses to tell me about the people they work, and have worked, for. I wondered if my experiences were unique. This is what I found out.

For the most part, restaurant owners and managers are idiots. The only difference between them is that managers walk like they have a cucumber up their butt.

Alexandra Lee
New York City

I think they are crazy. I think most of them are crazy.

Bob Dombroski
Orso
New York City

I think that restaurant owners and Muslims are the craziest people on earth. It's such hard work, it's such long hours, and you work under pressure all the time. There was an article in *The New York Times* about eight months ago where they calibrated the stress level for various professions and waiters came in second behind air traffic controllers. I don't think it's any better for owners. You set up a business, it's popular, you have a good business for a relatively short period of time because it's fashionable, because it's new and they want to try it out, and business reaches a kind of level. If you buy the food you're up at four or five in the morning to go and buy the produce, and you're at the restaurant until midnight or later. The guy I work for does that, although he doesn't need to because he has people he employs to manage the place. But he doesn't trust them. That's the whole thing about being a restaurant owner; you don't trust anyone. You are worried that the waiters are ripping you off, the managers are ripping you off, and the customers are ripping you off. We had a person sitting up at the bar having a piece of fish a few weeks ago. We're primarily a fish restaurant. Marvin, the owner, goes to the fish markets four or five times a week, and has the head chef go the other two times—otherwise he'd fall down and have a heart attack. The point being that Marvin knows what he's talking about as far as fish is concerned. So this woman was sitting down having this meal and she said the fish wasn't fresh. And Marvin had just purchased it that day. He went tearing off to the kitchen and pulled out this tray of whatever kind of fish it was and ran through the dining room out to the bar and stuck this whole tray of raw fish under this woman's nose and said, "SMELL THESE! THERE'S NOTHING WRONG WITH THESE!" You're working on your nerve endings the whole time, and it's certainly not a healthy environment to work in. It's smoke filled, the kitchen is as hot as hell. I'd like to see the longevity figures on people who work in restaurants—I'm sure they die earlier than most normal people.

Chico Garcia
Midnight Lake
New York City

I hate to make a generalization, but I would say that about 80 percent of restaurant managers are assholes on some kind of a power trip. I don't trust them, and I think they are two-faced. Actually, where I work now they are okay. But they can always turn against you. I don't think there are many restaurant managers who are straightforward, who tell you where you stand and what is going on. If they don't like you, or they don't like the way you look, they don't tell you. They just start maneuvering to turn the tide against you to get you out. It's very manipulative. You've had the same schedule for six months and all of a sudden you don't have Friday night. They play with your money. I don't trust restaurant managers with the time of day.

Dan Shapero
San Francisco, California

I have worked for some managers who were pretty fair, but I have found that this business seems to be a magnet for people who are on ego trips or who have a real need to dominate and call all the shots, even if it's unfair. It's funny because probably one of the most blatant cases is somebody who was supposed to be my friend. In the course of working with me he was always coming up and putting his hands all over me, or trying to practice the Heimlich Maneuver on me. And I would have to say, "Excuse me, those are my breasts. Will you stop?"

Bridget Munger
Arthur's Landing
Weehawken, New Jersey

Most managers I've worked under border on the desperate. Most owners have forgotten along the way how their restaurants are supposed to run. I had a manager who was a beeraholic; we would get beer deliveries every other day. He was sweet and would get maudlin when he saw it was slow and we weren't making any money. He'd stuff $50 in our tip cup and want us to drink with him while we were still working. He once bought another waiter a pair of Doc Martens because his were red and against the rules. He was taking all this money from the register. Moondance belonged to Greenpeace that year, the Cancer Society, the ACLU. . . .

Cherie Hamblin
Moondance Diner
New York City

Jackson Hole Wyoming was a tight ship. If you did one thing wrong, or out of order, your job was in jeopardy. You started as the new waitress, and you had certain responsibilities as the new kid. Then when you moved up to the next-to-the-newest you had other responsibilities. Like you could never take a phone order until you were at least third from the top of the echelon. And if you ever messed up and didn't fess up you had to walk a really thin line. They were very nice to you, and you made really good money, but one false move and you were one step away from oblivion. So you constantly had to cover your butt. Not that I ever had to cover my butt, but I did go into oblivion—I was fired. It's the only place I've ever been fired from. I was away for the weekend, this was over a Fourth of July weekend, and the day I was coming back I was flying standby on People's Express. This was back in the '80s, and I wasn't sure I could get a flight. So I had covered my shift for the next day with the #1 head waitress, who had worked her way up the corporate ladder at Jackson Hole Wyoming stepping on heads and kissing butt all the way up. Well, she decided at the last minute that she couldn't do it and didn't replace herself. She called them and blamed it on me, essentially, when in fact it was her fault. I came in to work the next day and worked the entire shift and they were very nice to me. I'm Greek, and so I really loved them because they were this cool old Greek family from Queens. Anyway, as I was walking out the door Mr. Pete, who was the father, and old, he was in his sixties, said, "Cyndi," and I turned around. It was like The Godfather. He was sitting on this barstool and I said, "Yeah, Mr. Pete?" and he said, "You're fired." It was so bad. I said, "Look at me and say that." I was pissed. And he wouldn't look at me. And everybody else who worked there had disappeared; they had all known I was getting it. And I had made friends with these people. So I started to walk out the door and I thought, I'm fired, I have nothing to lose, and I really liked this man so much, so I turned around and I walked back in and I said, "Mr. Pete, I know you won't look at me while I say this, but I just want to tell you that I loved this job. I know I did a really good job. I can't believe you're firing me for something that is not my fault and you didn't bother to ask me about it. It's been great working for you, but you just made me lose my respect for you by not looking me in the eye." And I walked out the door.

> Cyndi Raftus
> Hourglass Tavern
> New York City

The last restaurant I worked at in Austin was a great place to work because the waitstaff basically ran the restaurant. The owner/manager had a heart of gold but had no restaurant savvy. He was an example of a guy who shouldn't have been in the restaurant business. Fortunately, it was his wife's family's money. They shelled out the dough and they had to suck it up. Their son-in-law was a dipshit; he should have stayed in the army.

Now I work for a corporation, and that's totally different. They own thirteen restaurants in the Bay Area and the head office is right upstairs from us. So it makes things a little more tense for us. On the other hand, I've never heard of a job waiting tables where you get full medical and dental benefits like we do. Also, we can take up to six people to any of the restaurants and get 50 percent off the total bill. So it's a great company to work for.

There's one thing about restaurant management I should mention. Cocaine has been the downfall of almost every restaurant manager I have ever worked under. I could tell you horror stories. In 1985, I was working at this restaurant in Austin, Texas, and at the time there was a lot of money in Texas; it was really rocking. The manager of the restaurant was this insane guy. He was a hard worker, but he just loved to do blow. One minute he'd be your best friend and the next minute he'd be threatening to fire you. One evening he had plans to fly to Dallas at eight o'clock to hang out with Willie Nelson. He was a huge Willie Nelson fan and somehow he had hooked it up to be invited somewhere where Willie was going to be. So it started snowing. It was this freak thing, but it was great that it happened. Anyway, it started snowing and he couldn't get a flight out. He was a wreck. So I was taking this order at a table. It was three guys and they ordered two Cokes and an iced tea. As I'm walking to the bar to get the Cokes he comes up and says, "Did you check their IDs?" and I said, "Mac, they're drinking Cokes," and he says, "Don't talk back to me." I said, "You asked me a question," and he said, "Punch out." I'm thinking, man, this guy's a total freak. So I said, "Look, I've got work to do okay?" About fifteen minutes later I'm coming out of the kitchen with a big tray of food and he says, "I thought I told you to punch out." And I said, "Look. *You* punch out, *I'm* working. We're on an hour wait here, it's Saturday night, and I'm busy," and he storms off. It's getting close to eleven o'clock and there's still a line of people waiting to eat. I'm taking a check up to the cashier and I see Mac; his eyes are lifeless like a shark, just black as coal. He must have done every bit of blow that he had left. He comes up to me and he says, "What are you still doing here?" and I said, "I work here."

He grabs me by my neck and slams me into the cigarette machine. All the people in the restaurant are looking on and he says, *"You son of a bitch."* He had this little piece of shit office with no windows in the basement and he tells me to come down there. I get down there and he starts choking me. He's screaming, "I'M GONNA KILL YOU, I'M GONNA KILL YOU." I pulled his hands away from my throat and I handed him my checks. I said, *"You* wait tables, I'm out of here," and I started to leave. He catches up with me and says, "No. You can't punch out, you've got work to do." I said, "You're a total psychotic." About fifteen minutes later he gets a call that the airport has reopened, and he starts kissing my ass. He calls me from the airport and says, "Look, I'm sorry. Don't tell the owner and everything will be okay," but I quit after that. That guy caused so much hell for everybody there. We used to go round and round.

> Dickie Mallison
> MacArthur Park
> San Francisco, California

As long as they don't have temper tantrums, or throw adding machines or bottles at you they're okay.

> Dimitri Rathschech
> New York City

The restaurant I work in now is owned by two young, fairly intelligent, well-educated people who treat the waitstaff with a lot of respect. We've all been there forever; we're like one big dysfunctional family. These people trust us, so they're not always breathing down our necks. But I have worked in restaurants where the manager is just an idiot on some kind of a power trip. And they know how stupid they are, and they know you know how stupid they are, but they don't want to admit it.

> Doug V.
> Los Angeles, California

I have general views about them. I was talking to my wife about it this morning. She's in restaurant management now for a big hotel chain so she has layers and layers of these idiots above her. And she also waited tables a good long time, so she's been on both sides. It's hard to believe the kind of people that restaurants hire for management. I look at it as the inherent arrogance of the people at the top. Especially in corporate chain restaurants. They think they know exactly what is going on even though they don't spend more than an hour and a half a month in the place. They believe they know everything, and it leads to bad decisions and second-guessing. Waiters have nothing better to do than second-guess management, and we're always right. The people at the top don't see it on the front lines every day.

My wife runs the Friday and Saturday night shifts at this restaurant in a hotel. There is this huge hierarchy—general manager, kitchen manager, manager on duty, etc.—and they sit around at these meetings and say, "What's wrong with Friday night? What can we do to make Friday night better?" No one thinks to ask her. She's there on Friday night for ten hours, sees the clientele, deals with the staff, and they think they have all the answers. And this is inherent in every restaurant. How many times have you seen some big decision come down from above when no floor staff was ever consulted? They have this arrogance, and ultimately it hurts the restaurant.

Garrett Harker
San Francisco, California

When I first went to Florida I worked at this place called Crawdaddy's, which is part of a chain. I was a cocktail waitress. It was obvious that the owner had never really *worked* in the restaurant business. He never actually spoke to us, but we were informed that he wanted to change our uniforms. He wanted us to wear lime green skirts that were so short that they would expose these lacy underwear, which were also part of this proposed uniform. On top we were supposed to wear a lace-up shirt that exposed a lot of cleavage and had puffy sleeves. It was sort of a Heidi-of-the-Alps look, in lime green. We all said we would walk out rather than wear those uniforms. And that's what I can't stand; when people who have never even been in the business try to run it. I think that people who run restaurants should have to wash dishes, bus tables, wait tables, and cook before they are turned loose on the staff, so they will know what they're talking about. I've done all those things, and I have a pretty good idea of how a restaurant really works.

I've worked at a lot of places, and I would say that I've worked with two good managers; the rest were ballbusters. The last place I worked in Florida the manager had the most foul mouth I've ever heard. She would stand in the kitchen expediting the food, screaming, "COME GET YOUR FOOD, YOU MOTHERFUCKERS!" And the kitchen doors would be swinging open. I know that the customers could hear her. I think managers should treat their waiters with respect; they will get better results if they do.

Stacey Jurewicz
Pescatore
New York City

Generally I think that restaurant managers are the most unhappy race of humans to ever be put on the face of the planet. You have to hate yourself and life so much to manage a restaurant. The thing about managers is that they don't make that much money. You have to work a million hours a week, you have all this responsibility, and you don't have the benefit of owning the place. So they are constantly stressing. And they hate all waiters. Because the minute something else comes along the waiters are out of there.

Gregg Ostrin
Beverly Hills, California

I think there are two kinds of managers. There are the kind that are hired as managers, who are just useless because they don't know what it means to be a waiter, and then there are the kind that claw their way up the ladder, and they're just evil.

Waiter X
Khin Khao
New York City

The guy I work for now is the best boss I've ever had. He's a great person and he really knows how to be a good boss. He's French, and his parents were restaurateurs. He has that European edict that the restaurant is family, and you're treated as such. You're treated as someone who has a full life, someone who has other interests. If you do your job well you are respected, not treated like a disposable servant. And he views the waitstaff as an important part of the restaurant. He's great because he lets us do what we need to do, and when we're overstressed he steps in and does exactly what needs to be done and never points it out, and never complains. He's really professional and really terrific. We have a nice personal relationship as well. Most of the staff has been there four or five years, which says a lot about the place.

Jennifer
L'acajou
New York City

Owners and managers are the worst. The ones I work for now are the best I've ever worked for and I'm really grateful to them. They take good care of me, they're really nice to me. I have health insurance, I get vacation pay, I always tell people how great these people are. As long are you're up front and honest with these people they are wonderful, and that is all you can ask for. But these people are the exception. Restaurants attract a lot of different kinds of people, but until this job most of the people I worked for had some kind of problem—they were manic, wired, or very temperamental. You couldn't say hello to some of the managers I worked for. What *is* that? I mean, I was raised to say hello to people, especially where I work, so to keep from being angry I would just not say a word until I was spoken to. You just never knew what they were going to do.

> Michael K.
> The Grill
> Beverly Hills, California

I've worked for fifteen owners, and I'd piss on every one of their graves. I've been lucky with managers. I come from a family where I was browbeaten by an authority figure, so for the first five years of waiting tables I was a cowering, little scaredy-cat. At Chez Pascal I worked for a manager who was the best maître d' I have ever seen. He was casual, cool, and calm with the guests, but he needed a whipping boy, and I was it. He let me have it. He would stand at the table, and if I wasn't pouring the wine just so, he'd scream in my ear in French. He would call me names that made the other waiters blush. He used to call me a female whore, and a piece of shit, and the customers could generally understand what he was saying. One day I said, "I'm going to go now," and quit. I left, and the next day he called me back. From that day on he loved me. And since then I have had good relationships with managers. I'm a good waiter, and I don't let them get to me. I've been lucky.

> Ted LoRusso
> Perretti's
> New York City

I worked at this place at the end of the strip in Virginia Beach. It's an institution. Year-round they have an ad in the want ads for waiters and waitresses because they are constantly being fired. Every single day somebody got fired. Sometimes two or three, or even more people. It's a huge place and they had seven separate dining areas. We called the owner Little Hitler. Every dining room had video monitors that would sweep the room. It wasn't because they were afraid a customer was going to walk out with a plate or something, it was to keep the waiters and waitresses in line. And he had eight screens in his office where he would just sit and watch. If a waiter or waitress was caught eating any food that came back they were fired immediately. He would either fire them on the spot or wait until their shift was over. He was so crazy. You got a minimal employee meal at the beginning of the shift, but there was no choice or anything. Like hot dogs. They would give you hot dogs and it was a seafood restaurant. You could only eat in this one area and you had to be done in ten minutes or something like that. And then if you got thirsty in the middle of the shift and you wanted to have a soda, or even a glass of water, you had to go to the host or hostess and get a chit, then go to the bartender and give him the chit—just because you're thirsty—and he would get you a Coke or a glass of water. Then you had to carry that Coke all the way through the restaurant to the kitchen. On the floor of the kitchen there was a square, outlined with that stuff that they make the lines on the road with, around four feet by four feet, and that was where you could drink your drink. That was the only place you could consume your beverage. I got fired. I was about ten minutes late one Sunday brunch. I was nineteen years old and I would go out to the bars on Saturday night and close them—that's what you do when you're that young. So I was a little groggy when I got up and I was ten minutes late. He let me work and then at the end of the shift he fired me.

> Michael Marx
> Jethro's Bar & Grill
> New York City

There seem to be two types of restaurant owners: the kind that are incredibly nice, and very giving, who let you just do your job, and the control freaks. I used to work for this woman in the Village who would always tell the customers, "Welcome to *my* restaurant, *my* restaurant." And if you ever had a disagreement with her she would say, "This is *my* restaurant, I'll do what I want." It was that control thing. She could also really go off and be a real tyrant. You had to be a real yes man. Yes, Jackie, my, you look beautiful today.

Michael Salmons
Braque
New York City

Restaurant owners are a strange breed. They're never happy, and they can never relax. I worked for one man who owned a successful restaurant and he was miserable all the time. Every minute he was afraid he was losing business, and of course he thought that all the waiters were ex-cons. He always thought the worst of us, and he thought that if he didn't come in and constantly crack the whip that we were going to put him in the poorhouse. He had us do so much side work it was unbelievable. I really think he would have had us paint the outside of the building if he thought we would have been any good at it. We cleaned the bathrooms—I had to get up on a ladder and clean the chandelier and the exit sign over the door. A lot of restaurant owners are penny-wise and pound-foolish. They'll spend a lot of money on a new sound system but they won't buy another rack of glasses. They just decide you can make do with the glasses you have. And at nine o'clock you have no glasses. They keep it just short of what you need. It's the most frustrating thing when you go to reach for something and it's not there. The customers have no understanding of it, and they shouldn't. They shouldn't have to be bothered with something like that.

Nancy Kelly
New York City

You go through more managers than anything else. A manager makes or breaks a place. The food is important, but we in the front of the house are the most important thing. I don't care how good your food is, if the presentation is bad you go out of business. If a manager walks in miserable, the whole staff is going to be miserable. A manager's attitude projects itself onto everyone else's.

I worked for a wacko owner in Florida. He was a Greek guy. He used to grab your ass all the time. I thought, he doesn't want to touch me—a Greek is going to mess with an Italian? I'll throw him through the roof. One waitress said, "Look, if he grabs your ass, turn around and grab his balls. I swear to you he'll never do it again." And this guy was an asshole, too. One time a guy came in and ordered french fries, so I put the order in the kitchen. The fries came up right away, and they were cold. I said, "I can't take these out, they're cold." The owner was standing right there and he screamed, "TAKE THOSE FUCKING FRIES OUT NOW!" It was the kind of place where if you bitched, you got fired. And I needed the job at the time, so I had to bite my tongue.

Becky Milici
Fama
Santa Monica, California

The manager here is always saying that he would rather hire waitresses who don't have boyfriends. He says he doesn't want the customers to see your boyfriend dropping you off out front and kissing you, or waiting for you at the bar, because they might just come here for *you*. I think that stretches the job description a bit. He wants us to be little entertainers. And if we have a big party coming in he'll tell the hostess to dress sexy. She's a model so she'll come wearing a dress that's totally see-through. It's weird.

The owners are strange, too. If it's a bad night they both look like their lives are shattering in front of their eyes. I think that's why the manager hardly comes in anymore. And he's the one who really knows about the restaurant business.

The owner of the last restaurant I worked at was horrible. He was a total hard-ass. He had no respect for anyone who worked there. He was always yelling at everyone; you didn't want to be in his path. You couldn't even talk to him. This was in Boston. I was glad to leave.

> Kelsey Geisler
> Trompe L'oeil
> New York City

They know nothing.

> Pietro Bottero
> The Dock
> Fire Island, New York

I owned my own restaurant in Brooklyn for ten years, so I usually got along well with management. I'm much more management mentality. I have never had a hard time with owners. I do have a hard time with owners who don't really appreciate what's going on on the floor. When they have never done it and they don't understand the intricacies of waiting on tables or taking care of customers, they just know about the books. Or they think it should be done by rote. Every night is different, and every customer is different.

> Ray Proscia
> Georgia
> West Hollywood, California

Owners of restaurants are just insane and they all have drug problems. If they're a man, they are always big babies and they date eighteen-year-olds and it's like, get a life. It's all about just making them feel important. It's amazing to me. When Isabella's was Bud's, the owners would hang out there all night and play these games. The restaurant had three levels, and they would sit up on the top level, which overlooked the dining room.

They would do a shot and throw the glass and the other guy was supposed to catch it. Well, invariably the glass would sail out into the dining room and land on one of the tables below, then smash on the floor. And customers would just be freaking out.

Robin Shipley
Granita
Malibu, California

Most of the managers whom I have worked for that are totally out there and are always messing with you are on drugs. I mean I've worked for managers who are coked out and lose their shit over little things. And usually it's because they're all screwed up on drugs while they're working.

Russell Dean Anderson
Miracle Grill
New York City

Managers have no sense of humor. I feel sorry for them unless their family owns the restaurant.

Sam K.
Rox
Beverly Hills, California

Restaurant owners and managers are dogs. Ninety-nine percent of the time you're hired on your looks. The rest of the world does function that way, too, but with waitpeople it's even worse. I don't look like a bombshell so it wasn't always easy for me to get a job. Once I worked at this place on the Upper East Side and they fired me because they said I was too busy working the room and I couldn't turn tables. Well, a couple of years later I needed a job again and I went back there and they rehired me. They had completely forgotten me. But I ended up getting fired again, so I was hired and fired at the same place twice.

One of the great restaurant management scams is trailing. Or how to get people to work for no pay. Trailing is when you go in on your first day and follow someone around and do all the work for them. I was trailing at this restaurant and I had waited on all the tables while the person I was trailing stood at the bar and smoked cigarettes. I had made a lot of tips. At the end of the day I said, "How much of this do I get?" and they said, "You don't get any, you're just trailing." And it was like $100. I said, "Wait a minute, I don't even have money to eat dinner," and they said, "Tough." So I went into the meat locker and stuck a five-dollar bill in my bra. And I'll be damned if they didn't fire me. They said I stole the money. And I said, "Five dollars, give me a break. You weren't going to give me anything. Fuck you." So that was a one-day job.

Syd Straw
New York City

I used to work for this manager who was a southern guy, he was a football coach from Virginia. If you were really busy he would come up to you in the kitchen—you'd be sweating, you'd be all panicked—and he'd say, "Hey, hoss, you in the weeds? You in the weeds, hoss?" and he'd just be smiling. That was his big line and he'd do it to all the waiters. Instead of trying to see how he could help you he'd just stand there and laugh at you. It's funny now, but it wasn't all that funny at the time.

Tom Andonian
Los Angeles, California

In the Weeds

Buried. Swamped. In the weeds. Lost. Doesn't sound very pleasant does it? There comes a time when you have more to do than you can possibly get done. We refer to this as being swamped, or in the weeds. In very busy restaurants this can happen every night, or several times a night. I hate to even think about it.

You see, only two things are certain in the dining room of a restaurant: all the guests will come at exactly the same moment (because people eat out at 8:00 or 8:30, or 9:00 or 9:30, not at 8:17), and the host or hostess will find a way to fill up the stations one at a time, instead of giving one waiter a table, then another waiter a table, and so on. This insures that you will be swamped again and again, because people take about the same amount of time to eat. Your guests will all finish and leave at the same moment, and you will fill up all at once over and over.

When one gets five, or seven, or ten tables within minutes of one another nobody is happy. Not the customers, not the chef, and least of all you, the waiter. All of a sudden you need to get twenty-five drinks. But it's not just twenty-five drinks, it's seven or eight orders placed individually, which total twenty-five drinks. It's many trips to the bar, it's a lot of paperwork; and the customers don't care about any of that (nor should they), they just want their drinks *now*. While you are doing that, the people at one table are stopping you to ask questions about the menu, another table needs to have some food wrapped up and wants their check, and the bell is ringing in the back because an order needs to go out to yet another table. Meanwhile, when you bring one of these tables their drinks the woman decides that even though she did order a martini, she would much rather have a glass of white wine. It's okay to send it back isn't it? And of course she expects that she won't be charged for it.

When this is going on in my station I begin to experience physiological manifestations of stress. I sometimes become short of breath, and frequently begin sweating. Usually another waiter will come up and ask what they can do. Most waiters and waitresses respond the same way, "I don't know where to begin," or, "It would take too long to tell you." Being in the weeds is like death; ultimately you face it alone. The problem is that you really can't explain what needs to be done—there is simply too much. The act of telling another person would take precious seconds that you could use to do the work, and to describe all the things you need to do would be to admit the enormity of the task you face.

Like nausea, it comes in waves. Once you get the drinks, you have to take the orders. Naturally, when you turn eight or ten orders into the kitchen at the same time they get pissed. To repay you, they make sure that all those orders come up at the same second. The bell sounds like a railroad crossing, and you feel like you've been hit by the train. Then everyone wants coffee and dessert at the same time. But no table ever orders all their coffee at once. Never. It's always, "Oh, that looks good. I think I'll have one after all." So you figure twenty trips to the back, minimum.

The next thing you know the checks go down, the change comes back, you bus the tables, you set them up, and it starts all over again.

It's all part of the job. And, of course, when you are busy you make more money. But it is a terrible feeling. I know that I dislike it for at least two reasons; first, I don't like to feel panicked, or out of control. Who does? There is always the fear, in every waiter's mind, that it will get so out of hand that you have no choice but to take off your apron and walk out the front door. The other reason is that I genuinely want to do a good job. I take pride in my work. I want to give my customers good service, I want them to have a nice time. When you are in the weeds it is hard to give everyone what they want when they want it, and that bothers me.

At work we often tell war stories about how busy we were and how hard it was. It is very funny after the fact. I asked the waiters and waitresses who I interviewed what it felt like to be in the weeds. Here is what they told me.

I have been driven to tears by rushes. I ask myself, "Why the hell am I doing this? I should just leave." You feel that there is no way that you can get through it, but you do, and you're relieved, and then you pray that another rush doesn't come along.

> Amy Packard
> New York City

At Moondance every customer can see that you're running around, so they get scared and try to be patient. I hate it when my face gets all red and my customers give me that pity look.

> Cherie Hamblin
> Moondance Diner
> New York City

You usually know right before it happens. Everything is going okay, and then your section is full. And you're doing the best you can do without, well, *running* is not allowed in a restaurant. So you gotta walk as fast as you can. It's like the manager is standing there with the whistle in his mouth like a lifeguard at the pool, "Section five, *no running*!" The first thing I do is go find my busser and say, "Please. I'll put the extra fifty cents in the envelope today but you gotta help me." And you just have to consolidate everything as much as you can. The worst thing about being swamped is that even though I'm just a waiter I take pride in my work. It's my job, it's a responsibility, and I don't like to give shitty service. Because it's embarrassing. I don't want people to come back and go, "Oh no, not him, this guy sucks," you know?

Dickie Mallison
MacArthur Park
San Francisco, California

I went to get a job at the Beverly Hills Hotel and they told me that they hadn't hired anyone in seven years. So I said thank you and I started to walk out. Just then another woman came running up and tapped me on the back. She said, "Don't leave, one of our waitresses had a heart attack yesterday. Can you start tomorrow?" I should have known what to expect—all of these women had their twenty-five-year pins. I was the youngest by at least fifteen years. Of course, none of them liked me. And it was the first job I ever had that I had to have a real waitress uniform. I had to buy waitress shoes, and a pink uniform with a white apron.

I was going to work in the Loggia, which is the breakfast room. At that time Power Breakfasts were becoming a big thing and they were getting a lot of overflow. So they were setting up the Polo Lounge for the overflow, and that was my station. I had to get up at 5:00 A.M. to get there at 6:00 A.M., then I would set up my tables and wait until the Loggia filled up. When the Loggia was full they would start to seat my station. It was hellish because I would be sitting there for two and a half hours falling back asleep. On Mother's Day the overflow was so bad that I had close to thirty tables. And since the Polo Lounge wasn't really designed to be a restaurant it was the farthest from the kitchen.

The kitchen itself was huge. It facilitated the Polo Lounge, the Loggia, the outdoor eating area, which was mostly the lunch place, room service, all the banquets, and the fancy gourmet restaurant. The way it was set up was that there was a cold pantry for salads and cold juices and stuff like that, and on the far opposite end was the fry station, for anything that was fried. In another part there was a place for timed eggs; if you needed timed eggs you had to drop them yourself. You always had to toast your own toast and bagels, and if you had to get pastry it was in yet another part of the kitchen. So I would have to run this long distance from the Polo Lounge to the kitchen and then run around from one area of the kitchen to the other to pick up different items for one order. And they also had those silver lids so you could stack plates on top of each other. You could sometimes carry eight plates on a tray.

On Mother's Day, as I said, I had thirty tables. Some of these old ladies started coming out of the Loggia to help me. Swamped isn't even the word—I don't know if you've ever heard this expression, but we used to say "in the weeds." I mean, I was in the *jungle*. I looked up and I said, "No. No, no, no!" They just kept on seating people. And these are people dressed up in their Sunday best and they're out for Mother's Day. They're not turning anybody away; there are tables so they are seating them. So these women are handing me pieces of paper— you know, "Here's table twelve, here's table six, here's table ninety-two. I don't know what that table is, it's over there." I couldn't read their writing. I'd get in the kitchen and have ten pieces of paper that I'm trying to decipher. Plus, you had to make dupes for each different station in this kitchen, right? I didn't know where I was or what I was doing. I would just gather as much shit as I could gather and run out the door. I was stacking the plates four-high, the tray would weigh about one hundred pounds. I lost it. I was crying uncontrollably. I would set the tray in the middle of the room and sob, "Blackberry pancakes!" and somebody would meekly say, "Over here, if it's not too much trouble." So two people would be served at one table and the other three wouldn't, and everybody could see the shit I was in so they were really nice to me. They were so happy that they got anything. I made a fortune. And I just kept on thinking, "I'm leaving, I'm walking out, I can't take this, I'm losing it." And it didn't stop—the old ladies just kept handing me these slips of paper. I still can't believe I didn't walk out.

Two days later the alarm went off and I just went back to sleep. My phone started ringing and I didn't answer it for three days. Finally, on the third day, I picked it up. They said, "What's the matter, how come you didn't come in?" and I said, "I'm having a mental collapse, and I quit."

Maryanne Contreras
Los Angeles, California

It's been a while since I've been in the weeds because this restaurant is so slow. But at Sunset Grill and Bar, in Boston, I was always in the weeds. It was a very high-volume place. I would occasionally get a little panicked, but the idea is for your customers not to know that. And you can get irritated. There are so many things you're not in control of in a restaurant; the kitchen can send out stuff that's not done right so it gets returned, which slows you down, and then they ask you a million questions, and it's like, "Who cares? Just make a new one!" All the little stuff can add up. But being busy is better than being slow.

Kelsey Geisler
Trompe L'oeil
New York City

My first waiting shift I almost started crying. I was paralyzed. I didn't know where to go next I was so lost. It was a busy Sunday brunch and everybody was yelling at me. Luckily, one of the tables that I really screwed up had a waitress sitting at it. She said, "This is your first day of waiting tables isn't it?" and I said, "Yes," and she told me what to do and that it would be over soon.

> Doug V.
> Los Angeles, California

The weeds? I've never been there, but I hear it's terrible. Watching the other waiters it doesn't look like any fun. To be honest, the restaurant I worked in out here wasn't ever all that busy. At Legal Seafood in Boston we were so busy that you knew there would be three or four times in a night when you'd be completely weeded. And all a waiter wants to know is that he's in control. Even if it's only his little four- or five-table station that he's in control of. When things are being passed down to you, and your customers aren't acting the way they should, that's when it sucks. And that's what makes people miserable and not be able to hack it as waiters. But sometimes it can be really good to be in the weeds. Sometimes it can be almost religious. You're so focused that you're not thinking about anything else; it's almost like some sort of meditative thing. Now maybe that's hindsight, maybe that's not exactly the way it is when you're going through it. I met my wife in a really busy restaurant and I don't think that was an accident. When you're weeded like that you let down your guard and you see who's an asshole and who's not. I saw my wife handle really difficult things without coming apart. I mean we all lose our cool, but then you see what kind of person someone is when the veneer is stripped away.

> Garrett Harker
> San Francisco, California

I love being in the weeds. I love not knowing what is going to happen next. A long time ago someone told me to treat my whole station as one table, and that's what I do. You don't get as far behind if every time that you do anything in your station you see if you can do it at all your tables. Like pour water, for instance. So I'm always good at doing everything I can at one time. And I like being really busy, it makes the night go by faster. You also make more money. One thing I do hate though, is that lull before you get busy. From about 5:00 to 7:00 P.M. You just want to go home.

Stacey Jurewicz
Pescatore
New York City

Being in the weeds is like being in a firefight and needing reinforcements and nobody is around. Your radio isn't working, you're out of ammunition, and you're surrounded. You reach this point of emotional meltdown where you're paralyzed with anxiety. It becomes a juggling act. I don't know how to apply it to other things, but I have developed this ability to monitor the complete goings-on at seven or eight tables simultaneously. I'm aware of what everybody needs and where everybody is at, and it becomes a muscle. And what is so funny is that when you are sitting at a table in a busy restaurant everything looks fine. But it's horrible.

Gregg Ostrin
Beverly Hills, California

You immediately get the sensation that everyone is pulling on your coattails. It happened to me last night. I got a four top and a ten top at exactly the same time. And then these people order eight bottles of wine. I have to get glasses and open all the bottles and the owner is running around saying, "Are you okay? Are you okay?" And then there's the chef who is screaming at me to expedite food—and I have no choice but to drop what I'm doing and run it out. There's just no way out. You just have to do one thing at a time and hope that people don't start working you. There is a sense of excitement to it. I'd rather be running around than sitting down twiddling my thumbs and folding napkins.

Dan Shapero
San Francisco, California

I'm really good at being in the weeds. I'm like, oh, I'm in the weeds, it's hopeless, I'll never get out. It's almost easier than being steady, because when you're steady you have time to think about how much you hate your work. It's all about having the right attitude. I've worked a number of jobs with my sister and it's great because we won't help each other. I'll get in the weeds really bad and she'll come up to me and go, "Weeds, weeds, weeds, weeds, weeds!" and it's actually a big help, because I'll realize that I was starting to care. But if you forget and start caring it's horrible. I have actually screamed in small rooms and run out of restaurants. I've kicked things. It's like the ninth circle of hell. It's like, what did I do to deserve this? What did I do?

Waiter X
Khin Khao
New York City

It's hell. Your head wants to explode. And it's hard because people want to help you but you can't let them. If you stop to explain what you have to do you lose everything that's on your mind. It's chaos, it's just hell. I hate it. And that's why I hate waiting tables.

Jackie Becke
Los Angeles, California

When you are in the weeds you just want to die. There have been so many times I have been on the verge of saying, "GET IT YOURSELF!" It's not to be believed. Because people get really angry. Some people are very patient and can sit back and wait till you get to them, and some people you can feel getting more and more angry, and that just makes you sweat more. It's the worst. We've been real busy a couple of times lately, but we haven't been swamped in a long time. Sometimes on a busy night you'll be in the weeds for twenty minutes or half an hour, and that's okay, but when you're like that all night long and you're turning tables and turning tables and everybody wants a bottle of wine, or a second bottle of Evian, or an extra napkin, and they want to change their order, it's hell. You just can't get it all done. As I've gotten older I've gotten less stressed out about it. I just tell myself that there's nothing I can do, I'm moving as fast as I can and I can't go any faster. I work with a woman who's a bit older and she has been a wonderful influence on me. When I get really stressed out she says, "Honey, calm down. They can wait."

Jennifer
L'acajou
New York City

In Daytona Beach there is a big Mexican restaurant right across the street from the Speedway where they hold the Daytona 500. It is a food machine. The menu ran from $5.95 to $12.95. Get them in, and get them out. Every night we'd have a two to two and a half-hour wait. Every night of the week. And you knew that at 6:45 you were going to be buried. Drugs were *encouraged*— you've got to keep up with it somehow. Waiters would drink about ten cups of coffee and do a couple of rails and come running out to their tables screaming, *"HOW ARE YOU DOING TONIGHT!"* One night I got so far behind that I just had to take a break. The tables weren't going anywhere. I'd get to this point where I'd just say, "Fuck it, it's chaos, there's no saving this thing, I'm through, I'm not going to make shit off these tables,

I'm gonna have a cigarette and drink a cup of coffee."
So I'm taking this break and the bookkeeper comes up
to me and says, "There's this guy on the phone and I
think he's asking for you." I said, "I'm busy right now,"
and she says, "I think you'd better come and talk to
him." I walk over to the bookkeeper's window and I pick
up the phone and say, "Hi, it's Matt, can I help you?" and
this guy says, "Yeah, I think you're my waiter. I'm sitting
down here by this big tree under the stairs and I need
some coffee." I just started laughing. I said, "No problem, I'll be right there." So I take the coffee to the guy
and fill his cup. A few minutes later he goes to the bathroom and I pick up his cellular phone and get the number off of it. I wait about ten minutes and I go to the pay
phone and I call this guy at his table. I say, "Hi. This is
Matt, your waiter, you need anything right now?" He
about died laughing. He ended up leaving me a tip that
was equal to the total of the bill. I had a blast with that
guy.

> Matt Jaroszewicz
> Gainesville, Florida

You don't know what to do next. That is when you
feel like taking your apron off and walking out the door. I
bet more waiters quit when they are in the weeds than at
any other time. I have actually been so deeply in the
weeds that I went upstairs and got changed; I was going
to leave. But then I thought, I can't do this to the other
waiters, so I put my uniform back on and went down and
got caught up.

> Ted LoRusso
> Perretti's
> New York City

I actually like it. I'm more organized when it's crazy.
When it's dead I start to fuck up. We have twenty-five tables each, and when it's really busy it's insane; everybody wants something every second and you have

walkouts that you have to chase down the street. It's great. But there are some waitresses that just lose it. It's my favorite time.

Shawna Mason
Lone Star Roadhouse
New York City

How does it feel to be swamped? Imagine you are stuck in a crowded subway car at rush hour. Everybody is sweaty, and there is no air-conditioning. You have no room to move or breathe, and the subway conductor announces that the train has to stop between stations indefinitely.

Naiem Mohammed
Museum Cafe
New York City

When you are new you're always in the weeds. One high-maintenance table can put you in the weeds. I love to be in the weeds. It's a challenge. But not where you're so far in the weeds that it makes you crazy. This restaurant I just left, it was all tray service. The kitchen was really far, I had the station that was the farthest away, and that kind of weeds I don't like. I like to be busy though—when I'm busy I make less mistakes. I feel like I'm on a roll.

We had a waiter in Boca who used to say, "Busy? I'm as busy as a whore on dollar day!"

Becky Milici
Fama
Santa Monica, California

I have a really keen knack of being able to prioritize, so if I have ten tables I can sweep through my station and take care of something at all of my tables. And the other thing is that I'm not at all reluctant to give a table away. If I'm really busy I'll give it to another waiter. I much rather they take the table and the people get good service. But when I actually get in the weeds it's sort of like being in a car and going down a really steep hill and not having any brakes. You know you're going to hit something, but you have no idea what it is. You're just completely out of control. And it's horrible being out of control, horrible.

Ray Proscia
Georgia
West Hollywood, California

We are always getting swamped, because these bus tours will stop and come in. All you can do is take one thing at a time and get the job done. All I know is that it takes me twenty-seven minutes to make sixty-two ice cream cones.

Rose Larsen
Rose's Den at the Boulder Inn
Milepost 28, Highway 93
Kingman, Arizona

It feels like you have five seconds to get to a bathroom that is five minutes away.

Sam K.
Rox
Beverly Hills, California

When I'm in the weeds it's like being underwater. I have so many things to do and I can't move fast enough. And I don't know what to do first. It just becomes panic. As I've been doing this longer it's not as bad, but when I was a rookie it was like a snowball, it would just get worse and worse. Recently we installed a computer in our place. Before that we were like the old McDonald's, everything was on paper and it worked. It worked like a charm. Then the computer came. On this computer there are a thousand spaces for menu entries, modifying orders, and various commands. We have a seven-page menu, so just to start we had 950 of these spaces taken up. The first Saturday night with the computer we were the busiest we had ever been. It was absolute mayhem. We didn't know the codes so we were just standing at the terminal going through the book trying to enter orders. Everybody got terrible service. The manager had to go from table to table apologizing. It was a feeling of complete hopelessness.

Tom Andonian
Los Angeles, California

You're on the floor from five o'clock to say, midnight, or one o'clock, and you're running the whole time. People are screaming orders at you the whole time, you have to remember half the stuff until you can get to a quiet place to write it down, the chefs are screaming at you because you're not getting the food out fast enough—I mean people are screaming at you the whole time—and you're always behind. You never have enough time to do everything you have to do. By the end of the night you're frazzled.

Chico Garcia
Midnight Lake
New York City

Hot flashes. It's like this sensation that comes up from your toes and you are on fire. And the worst is when people ask if they can help you and you're like, *"There's just too much to do. I don't know where to begin, I'd rather just sit here and drown."* And no one can understand. There are people screaming at you, and if you could sit down and explain what is really going on they would probably be pissed off anyway, so what's the point? I had a waitress when I was eating in a restaurant one time who just sat down next to me and started to cry. Just lost it. And people were looking at her and yelling, *"Excuse me. Where's my salad?"* I was like, "This woman's having a breakdown, okay? I'll get it for you." But that's one of the worst things about working in a restaurant: when you eat out you want to clear your own table. It's waiter guilt.

Robin Shipley
Granita
Malibu, California

The Chefs, the Cooks, and the Churlish

In an ideal world the separate parts of any business would work together harmoniously to achieve their mutual goal: customer satisfaction. As those of us who have ever been employed know, this isn't always the case. Take my business as an example. For many reasons, not the least of which is tradition, there is often a good amount of tension between the kitchen staff and the floor staff of any restaurant.

It would seem that the front and the back of a restaurant would want the same thing: loads of happy customers coming back to the restaurant again and again to turn their money over to us so that we can continue to enjoy our lower-middle-class existence. While this may be true in the abstract, our concepts of how to make this happen are frequently divergent. A good example is when a customer wants to create a new menu item. It used to be that people went to a restaurant because they liked the food on the menu. In the 1990s I think that customers view a restaurant as more of a supermarket with a cook; that they can sort of mix-and-match all of the ingredients in the building to invent a meal that they consider palatable. Understandably, the kitchen staff doesn't much care for this. First of all the chef's ego is involved; he or she has created the dishes on the menu to reflect his or her culinary vision—in the chef's mind it's like adding a few different colors to the *Mona Lisa*. Secondly, it's a pain in the ass. A restaurant kitchen is very much like an assembly line, they are trying to prepare many, many plates of food as quickly as possible and if all of the customers want their orders individualized it creates chaos. This makes for tension between the kitchen and the waitstaff because it is our inclination to give the customer pretty much whatever they want. The reality of our job is that if a customer is unhappy, whether it's with a restaurant policy (like no cigar smoking, for instance), or the time it takes for their food to cook, they reflect that unhappiness in the one way that they can—the tip. So we take all these special orders back to the kitchen, and the kitchen staff gets mad at us because it makes their job harder.

Another touchy subject between waitstaff and the kitchen is compensation. Kitchen workers are, in most instances, underpaid. Yes, executive chefs at four-star restaurants sometimes earn six figures. But the people who actually cook your food in those same restaurants, the people on the line, may be making $6 an hour. Really. Waiters generally make more than that. Of course when business is slow waiters make nothing. While it varies from restaurant to restaurant, I would say that the average waiter makes more money than the average cook. This breeds a bit of resentment. Cooks work very hard, there is no doubt about that. All the yelling and screaming alone must be exhausting. They deserve to make more money. But whose fault is that?

I first noticed that kitchen workers were a different breed at my maiden restaurant job. The cooks there had a favorite game. I can't remember what it was called, but I can tell you how it was played. Two guys would each get a side towel (a square cotton all-purpose rag) and wet it. They would then take turns popping each other's forearm with a whipping motion that produced an audible snap. There was only one rule to the game, and it determined the outcome—whoever first cried out was the loser. After one of these sessions both players would have large red welts on their arms. Sometimes they would even draw blood. Even though this game was great fun to watch, I must say I never had the desire to play.

My last job exemplified what I would call the traditional rift between the kitchen staff and the floor staff. At that restaurant the owner was the executive chef, which is to say that he planned the menu, ordered the food, and created the specials. The actual cooking during the evening was handled by two cooks—one who prepared salads and appetizers, the other who made the main dishes. I have found this to be a fairly common arrangement in New York City. In this case, the entire kitchen staff, with the exception of the executive chef/owner, was from a small village in Mexico. These guys were the nicest, most diligent people you could imagine working with, and they consistently turned out good food. The only problem was that from the day they arrived at the restaurant the owner would begin cultivating a waiter-hater mentality in them. He encouraged the kitchen staff to refuse to do any special orders, and generally treat the waitstaff with disdain. And of course we were required to treat the kitchen staff like gods. The owner actually hung a sign in the kitchen that told us to call out our orders beginning with, "Ordering please," and ending with, "Thank you." Now these are the kind of common courtesies you can pretty well expect from a waiter because we are a polite bunch. But to have someone require you to say please and thank you to a coworker for something as routine as turning in an order is an insult. As if they are doing us a favor by cooking the food. It's their *job*, for crying out loud. I use this kitchen as an example because it was the perfect control group—these guys came to our restaurant straight from a farming community in Mexico; they had no reason in the world (other than prompting from their boss) to dislike waiters. Their bad attitude toward us was actually cultivated by the executive chef.

I consider myself very fortunate, excepting the fact that I work in a restaurant at all, because we have none of this sort of discord at my current job. The kitchen and floor staffs get along very well on a personal level and actually work together as a team. Sadly, I think this is uncommon. I asked other waiters and waitresses to tell me about the chefs and cooks they had worked with. Here is what they said.

They are all on power trips. I think they all feel like they are cooks, and that they have to rise above that and be a chef by being an asshole. We have a wonderful one now, but for the most part they're condescending mamma's boys who like to play with their ovens and have to have this butch, powerful image.

> Bob Dombroski
> Orso
> New York City

I think in a lot of ways chefs have it worse than waiters. It's like working in the coal mines in Victorian England. It's always as hot as hell, you're working under pressure, and you have to have some kind of artistry to what you're doing. And most of the chefs I have known have been very, very aggressive. I've walked in the kitchen with an order at 12:10 when the kitchen closes at 12:15 and they started throwing crockery at me. I go back to the manager and say, "You know, there's cups and saucers flying around every time I walk in the room," and he says, "What do you want me to do about it?" By that stage they're so over it that there is no point in trying to confront them or they're going to get *really* aggressive. I mean they're just throwing stuff behind you, and you hope to hell they don't throw and hit you in the head.

> Chico Garcia
> Midnight Lake
> New York City

Chefs are wacked. They are out of their trees. What is it, the pressure? Maybe I'd operate the same way, I don't know. I deal with a chef right now who is a real Jekyll and Hyde. You can't do anything right with him— you're damned if you do and you're damned if you don't.

He's belligerent, he screams at his sous chef and everyone along the line. I'm amazed that somebody hasn't taken a boning knife and plunged it into his gut—I know I would have. It's all very arbitrary. You can just be walking by and he'll yell at you. What a dick. I don't understand the pathology of a chef. I don't know what they teach in culinary school. Maybe they hold their hands over a burner so they know what a fish being sautéed feels like, I don't know what goes on there.

Dan Shapero
San Francisco, California

Most chefs I have worked with have been male and have enjoyed their power. I worked with a crazy Filipino named Henry who was a great cook, but he drilled a hole in the back of the kitchen wall into the ladies' room. He looked like a tan Charlie Chaplin and had a bellow for a laugh. He hated this one waiter so much, for no discernable reason, that he would put roaches in his staff meals. He once put a live mouse at the bottom of this waiter's bowl of pasta—it jumped out and ran up his shirt. But Henry couldn't be fired. I think it was because the rest of the kitchen was related to him.

Cherie Hamblin
Moondance Diner
New York City

I don't know how he got the gig, but our chef is twenty-three years old and he's just a prick. He's got a huge attitude and it's hard to deal with. Especially when I'm as much older than him as I am. It's odd, because as you get older as a waiter your tolerance level actually goes *down*. You just don't put up with that kind of shit anymore. You're not gonna take it from a punk like that. But the chef has you by the nuts, you've got to do what he says or you hit the road.

Dickie Mallison
MacArthur Park
San Francisco, California

One time at a French restaurant in L.A. that I worked at a chef got angry with a busboy and started going after him with his knives—he started throwing them at him, and then he tried to beat him up. It took three of us to hold him back.

Dimitri Rathschech
New York City

At Madeleine the kitchen was all Thai. They wanted the women to be somewhat submissive, which I can't do. They also didn't want any talking in the kitchen. It was hard. At the place where I work now, the head chef just left. He had really long hair, and never wore a hairnet. In fact, he was hairy all over. Anyway, he would be on the line with a cigar in his hand. The whole time. And cigarettes, too. He always smoked while he cooked. One time he served a trout with a cigarette in its mouth. He had set it down on the shelf above, or something, and it evidently fell onto the plate. At any rate, this trout went out with a cigarette in its mouth. And that's also how it came back.

Stacey Jurewicz
Pescatore
New York City

Spago inspired me to go to cooking school. I had never been interested in cooking in a restaurant until I worked there. At Spago they were doing all these interesting things that I had never seen before. So I went to school, and when Wolfgang opened Eureka I got a job there; first as a prep chef, and then on the line. It was my revenge, because as a waiter I hated to go up to the line and say, "Could you make the veal chop with the fish sauce?" The cooks would always give me such a hard time and I would end up saying, "It's not for me. It's *them*; they asked for it. They're putting me up to it." Waiters are always victimized by these hot-headed chefs. So when I started cooking the waiters would come up to me and say, "Maryanne, can you do this, can you do that?" and I'd say, "Yeah, sure," or, "I can't do it right this second, it's going to take a little extra time, but yes, I'll do it." I also fed the waiters better than normal and I didn't take my frustrations out on them.

Maryanne Contreras
Los Angeles, California

I find that chefs are some of the hardest-working people I have ever come across and probably the most underpaid for the amount of work they do. In California many of the kitchen staffs are all Latino, and these guys are incredible people. We all kid around with the kitchen and it's a constant tension release. I come in to work and the chef will say, "Oh, are you working today? I quit." If you don't have that kind of release in a restaurant you'll see people breaking down, you'll see waitresses crying, you'll see all kinds of stuff. But we carry on and crack jokes, and it makes it so you can tolerate the bullshit you have to put up with.

Tom Andonian
Los Angeles, California

The chef I work with now is two or three years younger than I am and actually we get along fine. Of course we scream at each other all night long. He's under a lot of stress. He's a stressful person. But he'll change his tune to make whatever point he's trying to make. He was on a big tirade the other day that the waiters aren't pushing the specials hard enough. He said, "I make these specials, you have to spend a lot of time describing these specials at the table." The very next night one of the waitresses sold a special, a shrimp pasta. At the preservice, where the waiters got to look at the dish, it had four pieces of shrimp on it. When she brought it to the table it only had three. She said, "What in the hell is going on here?" and the chef said, "Molly, I wish you wouldn't tell the people how many shrimp are on the pasta." I can see it now; the customer asks, "Can you tell me how many shrimp are on the pasta?" "No, it's a secret. You can only find out if you order it. I know, the chef knows; you can't know."

Doug V.
Los Angeles, California

I've had my problems with chefs. I demand perfection. They'll throw the food up looking bad and I won't serve it. I've told them, "You get paid no matter what, I only get tips," and we go back and forth, back and forth. Because people will find a reason not to tip. They'll eat the whole thing and then say, "I didn't like it." I'll say, "What part didn't you like? *You ate it all.*"

The last guy I worked for was the best. He was the chef and the owner. Not one of those plates went out of the kitchen without looking tops. There was no saying, "Sorry, I'm not serving that." I've had that experience more than once. There were no problems.

Becky Milici
Fama
Santa Monica, California

My experiences with chefs have all been positive. I'm kidding. I think chefs are pretty much a hopeless breed. My wife went to culinary school and she told me that they go in day one as idiots. They're not bred in culinary school, it's not taught in the restaurant business, they're just fools to begin with—and then they're fools with power. Fools who feed people. And in a few years it's even worse. One of the things I've always liked about the restaurant business is the antagonistic relationship between the cooks and the waiters. It's so much fun. Because for the most part they have no grounds for their dislike of waiters. It's sort of like the customers; chefs are convinced that whatever goes wrong, whatever failings they might have in their careers, waiters are behind them. Every chef I have known has been like that.

My wife actually told me that in culinary school the instructors would tell them, "Watch out for your waiters. The waiters will screw you," and give no basis for that opinion. And my wife would say, "Wait a minute. I thought that the kitchen and the waiters were on the same team. Don't you *need* your waiters?" and they would tell her, "No. No way. *You don't need waiters!*"

Garrett Harker
San Francisco, California

If a chef is really good and knows what he's doing with the food, and has equal respect for the people on the floor, then he's fine. I generally find them to be miserable people. Really nasty, miserable people. The chef here busted my hump for the first six months that I worked here. He just treated me like shit. But then the owner went away for a month and I took care of the place and he realized that I was serious about the job and I knew what I was doing. He's been fine ever since. Plus, I gave him my free five miles off my pack of Marlboros and he's happy.

In general I think that chefs look down on waiters. Because in many circumstances I think waiters make more money than chefs. And they feel that it's very easy to be a waiter—that all you have to be able to do is walk and speak. And being a chef is difficult, there is a lot of discipline and training involved. So the money breeds some resentment.

Gary Chiappa
Roettele A.G.
New York City

I've always had really good luck with chefs. I think it's because chefs like good waiters who don't make mistakes. And since I grew up in an alcoholic household I don't make mistakes. Of course that's also why I'm a waiter. So all the chefs I've worked with have always liked me. There is the moody thing; all chefs get moody.

But I'm a big queen, so I can say, "Oh girl, you're so *moody* today!" and run out with the calf's liver.

Waiter X
Khin Khao
New York City

I get along great with chefs. You *have* to get along great with them. They're the ones who make your food, and if you don't get along with them they'll hold it up—I've seen them do it. I've always made it a point to become friends with them.

Jackie Becke
Los Angeles, California

They're a real bad lot. I've worked with some really difficult chefs and have managed to get along okay with all of them eventually, but they really are like the queen bee. I respect that in a certain sense because if the food is good my job is easier. And if the food being good means that the guy has to be a real asshole, then I guess that's the way it is. They are in a very high stress job as well, and sometimes I have a hard time appreciating that, because when there is a rush in the dining room they are crazy for forty-five minutes and we're crazy for three hours. And they don't understand that either; they wonder why we're still crazed when they've been standing around picking their teeth for an hour.

Jennifer
L'acajou
New York City

I think chefs are crazy. I think they're crazy, crazy people. Insane. It's a power thing. And they're really, really competitive. Plus, they're cutting up dead animals all day—it's not a good thing. They are under extreme pressure in the evening, and they're all alcoholics. They vent a lot on the waiters and try to belittle them all the time. Part of it is that they resent that waiters make more money than they do, or as much as they do. Waiters work really hard. I know that being a chef is a big responsibility, but they tend to turn into prima donnas sometimes.

Freeda Kaufman
Jethro's Bar & Grill
New York City

I worked with this guy named Bosco, and one night he was really busy and one of his orders died in the window. So he tells the chef he can't take the food out because the plate isn't hot. Never, never say that to a chef. The chef says, "Oh, is that what the problem is? No problem." Bosco walks out of the kitchen and the chef picks up a plate and puts it in the oven for about ten minutes. Then he plates up the food and rings the bell about ten times. Bosco comes running back in the kitchen and grabs the plate and burns the shit out of his fingers. He had blisters for about two weeks after that.

Matt Jaroszewicz
Gainesville, Florida

At Rakel the chef was co-owner. And Thomas Keller was the most anal person I have ever, ever met, period. Let alone worked with or for. Oh, God, was he anal. Everything in that kitchen was spotless. They had to wash the walls every night. It was a new kitchen; it had been built for that restaurant because it was a bank before that, so it was a beautiful, beautiful kitchen. They spent so much money on that kitchen. It had beautiful white tiles, stainless steel everything, and it was an open kitchen so he could stand there and look out into the dining room. You know, he *ruled*. And every single night his poor staff would have to scrub that thing down when they broke down the kitchen—the stoves and everything. The hood had to be done every night. It couldn't have any grease on it—nothing. Even the bottom of the pans, you know how at home your pans will be all black on the bottom? His were spotless. He was a horror. A horror.

Michael Marx
Jethro's Bar & Grill
New York City

Mostly chefs are maniacs. High-strung. I think most of them take it very seriously, no matter how bad the food may be. They think this art thing is going on.

Michael Salmons
Braque
New York City

I've worked with insane chefs, crazy chefs. I worked with a brunch chef once, and brunch is a phenomenon I don't understand—it's a circus; I think it's sloppy, disgusting, awful, sweaty, I don't know why anybody goes out for brunch in New York, but this chef had a terrible time with eggs. They would be returned because they were cold. The bacon would be cold, or something would be returned because it was overcooked, and he would refuse to recook things for us as though we were just doing this to antagonize him. Once I took an order back and he said, "I'm not recooking this order." The customer had said the French toast was burnt and the bacon was cold. What do I do? I'm all alone, there's no owner or manager around and the chef has said, "Fuck you, I'm not redoing this order." I wound up going to the bartender and he went into the kitchen and cooked it himself. The chef just made room for him. Didn't say anything.

I worked with a chef at Isabella's who was a fanatic, a real stickler for detail. I found out what he wanted and obeyed his rules and became one of his favorite waiters, but I think I almost gave myself an ulcer over it. I really did it at the expense of my health and well-being. We had a computer system that was loaded with modifiers for any kind of substitution or any specific instruction for food, and the chef told us repeatedly, "I don't want to see you. I don't want you to come down here and talk to me, I don't want to see your faces, I want you to punch everything into the computer." So we had several pages of modifiers that we had to punch into the computer in code. You'd be standing at the computer reading, turning pages, trying to find the code for dry, no spices. He wanted a complete story on the computer printout so he knew exactly what to do and didn't have to look at you. It was like the army.

Nancy Kelly
New York City

When I owned my own restaurant I went through maybe twenty chefs in ten years, half of whom had an alcohol or drug problem. And I've done everything, I've worked in kitchens, I've washed dishes, I've bussed, I've tended bar, and I certainly understand why people in that side of the business would be as addictive as they are. You're trapped in a small space. As a waiter I get to move around; I get to leave the heat of the kitchen and go into the dining room, I get to vent to the customers to a certain extent. But the chef is stuck in that hot kitchen turning out plate after plate and making sure every one is perfect. That's hard.

Ray Proscia
Georgia
West Hollywood, California

There is always a barrier between the kitchen staff and the floor staff in every restaurant. I'm friends with the cooks at my restaurant; we go out after work and everything. But then it all changes when we're working. One of them is really laid-back, and the other one is completely crazy. As in most restaurants, I think the kitchen staff sees itself as the backbone of the business, that they are the reason why people come in, and that they don't get enough respect for that. And then they get pissed off at us for making little mistakes, for not putting the time or the table numbers on the checks, for instance. One night they got mad at me because I tripped over a box on the floor of the kitchen and dropped a couple of plates of pasta, which they had to cook again. Who cares? There was a box on the floor and I tripped over it. It was an accident. I just walked out of the kitchen. I knew the dishwasher would clean it up so I just went back out front. I mean, it pissed me off that there was a box there in the first place.

I talked to the executive chef once; I told him that one of the cooks was crazy and he needed to calm down. He said, "They're hot, don't take it personally." And you can't. You just have to smile and walk away.

Kelsey Geisler
Trompe L'oeil
New York City

Chefs can be a joke. In one restaurant where I worked I was the only waitperson who could win the respect of the chef because I had the ability to talk like a foul-mouthed truck driver. Sad, huh? I avoid any kitchen because I always seem to get grabbed going through.

Robin Maynor
Linn's Fruit Bin
Cambria, California

I've had a chef threaten to beat me over the head with a pan, and I've had one ask me out on a date; they run the gamut. But they are the most temperamental men and women on the face of the earth. And this city has made the chef a celebrity. I think it's about time they made the waiter a celebrity.

The first thing I do when I start at a new restaurant is make friends with the chef. And that's the only time I'll ever bend over backward to get along with someone in a restaurant. The chef is the one guy who can really fuck you up. If he wants to hold that order, he will. You can't explain to him that the customer comes first—*he* comes first. If a customer's food takes a long time, they think it's my fault. They think I took their food and put it on the top shelf and that I will get to it when I can.

Ted LoRusso
Perretti's
New York City

In Los Angeles being a chef is a great way to get laid. It definitely is. They are such a rare breed. I think they are these misfits in society, ex-Deadheads and things like that, and they don't know what to do so they become chefs. Like the head chef at this restaurant is this big guy from Brooklyn who scratches himself all the time. And he's making pretty food. It's the weirdest thing. It's like someone told him that he could meet girls this way so that's what he's doing. Plus, chefs are stars in Los Angeles. They can get anything. It's very prestigious. They are *stars*. In New York they are known within a small circle; here it's a big deal. Especially if you're in Wolfgang's group. And they make *no* money. I mean, the head chefs do, but the guys behind the line make $6 an hour. It's incredible.

Robin Shipley
Granita
Malibu, California

I've been pretty lucky, but I worked for an owner-chef who was just loopy. He was just insane. He would make waitresses cry and stuff. He was a hot chef at the time, and Madonna and Sean Penn would come in, and Jay McInerney, and all these celebrities. It was a restaurant called Melrose. And the chef was a lunatic. I was the expediter and my job was to take the blame for any mistake that happened in the restaurant, even if it was his mistake. He put his plates out hot, and he was really anal about the presentation of the plates—which is fine. We would carry the plates with towels and tell all the customers that the plates were hot and to be careful not to touch them. One night I set a plate down in front of Daryl

Hall and he burned his finger on the plate after I told him not to touch it. He turned to me and said, "I'm leaving, I'm not paying for my dinner," and walked out and got into his limousine. The chef ran out of the kitchen with his knife and tapped on the window of the limousine with it, and when the window came down he pointed the knife in the guy's face and said, "Don't you ever set foot in my restaurant again, you baby." He was a lunatic, but his food was a work of art. On the other hand, it's just food.

Russell Dean Anderson
Miracle Grill
New York City

Nightmares

I just woke up from a nap. I was out late last night and had to get up early so I did something very unusual, I laid down for an hour in the early afternoon. While I was sleeping I had a nightmare. I was waiting tables in a restaurant I had never seen before. I wasn't sure where the kitchen was, I couldn't find the bar, and the dining room was an L-shape so I couldn't see all the tables that it was my responsibility to wait on. In my dream the restaurant was busy. Very busy. So busy, in fact, that they were bringing tables up from the basement and seating guests at them out on the sidewalk in front of the building. I was in a panic because I was the only waiter. More and more people were being seated and I couldn't get to them all—which on one level was okay because when I did get to them they were ordering drinks from me and I didn't know where to go to have them made. In the middle of all this I scratched my right wrist on something sharp in the restaurant (this is something that happens to me almost every night at work, I always come home with a cut, a scratch, or a bruise). The next thing I know my wrist and hand are beginning to swell and I am experiencing considerable discomfort. To make matters worse, I am right-handed, so now I can't write the orders that I don't have time to take. I decided that the best thing to do is to go home. I looked around for the host/manager and found, to my surprise and relief, that this dream restaurant is being run by Michael Howett, one of the owners of the restaurant where I work in my conscious life. Michael is one of the most decent people I have ever met, and the first sane restaurant owner I have ever encountered. But there are two things about Michael that are central to this dream: he knows how to seat a room to absolute maximum capacity (his motto is, "Shove 'em in, it'll stretch."), and he never panics. So when I showed my swollen, discolored hand to him he told me to run some cold water over it and see if the swelling would go down. I managed to find the bathroom and did just that. Unfortunately, the hand returned to somewhere near its original size so I was obliged to stay at work. Of course, when I returned to the dining room I was substantially more behind. At this point I woke up, sweaty and poorly rested.

I have had dreams like this since I first started working in restaurants. When I was fourteen I was a busboy. Frequently I would dream that I had somehow forgotten to bus the last table. This was an awful dream because the man I worked for at that restaurant would fire you without a thought if you neglected any part of your job. There were no second chances. A year later, when I was promoted to a waiting position, the waiter's nightmares began.

My work dreams are always similar, and they all have familiar components: I'm in a restaurant I have never seen before, I'm the only waiter, I can't see the entire dining room, the place is full, every customer wants something from me and for many reasons I can't get them what they want or even find the time to ask them what it might be, and they all hate me. In short, my nerves are about to snap. It's about stress and anxiety.

Maybe everyone has work nightmares. Maybe cashiers in

supermarkets in New York dream that their registers break down and they have to make change in their heads, or that they have to say thank you. Maybe CEOs have nightmares that their salaries will become tied to their performance. Who knows? All I know is that I resent dreaming about my job. You shouldn't have to take a job like mine to bed with you.

In speaking with other waiters and waitresses I was not surprised to learn that almost all of them have nightmares about waiting tables. What did surprise me was the different shapes that these dreams take. The mind is an incredible thing.

I have waiting dreams all the time. Usually they are about being swamped and not being able to accomplish anything. I can't get the coffee out and I can't get the menus to the tables. One day I had a problem with a really horrible woman who wanted poached eggs in her scrambled egg burrito and that night I had a nightmare about poached eggs. The effect that customers have on us is atrocious.

Amy Packard
New York City

There's this creep English punk rock guy with speedbumps all over his face. He just walks up and down Melrose Avenue all day long, he's been doing it for years. I had a dream he was in Mel n' Roses at table twenty-seven. In the dream I walked past him and noticed he was having a wank under the table. He came in the next day and sat at table twenty-seven and looked at me like he *knew*.

Cara Green
Swingers
Los Angeles, California

I'm prone to the stress dream every once in a while—too many things to do, panic, yelling at customers, dropping things, all of which I have *never* done in real life. I did have an unsettling sexual dream once that involved an older artist who always comes in for scones in the morning. I couldn't look him in the face for days afterward.

Cherie Hamblin
Moondance Diner
New York City

I used to have nightmares, but I don't anymore. Once you take control, all that is over. You have to let your customers know that you are managing the situation. And they will thank you for it. Every night at least two of my tables tell the manager that I gave them great service. I make them do it. They will thank me and tell me they thought the service was great, and I'll say, "Did you really think so? Then tell the manager."

I used to have nightmares a lot. I would have tables in Idaho, and I was in California. I would dream that I had to take a train to get to my tables, but the train wouldn't come. And the food would start to go bad, but I couldn't get the train. It was that vast.

Ted LoRusso
Perretti's
New York City

I still have these dreams where I'm swamped. You know, they seat you with two parties of twelve and three other tables at the same time, and you just can't handle it. I waited tables for ten years, and I quit waiting tables seven years ago, and I still have dreams about it. I dream that I'm the only one in the whole restaurant and I have to take all the orders, make all the drinks, and then run back and cook all the food myself. And then I come out and there's more people lined up around the block.

Maryanne Contreras
Los Angeles, California

My classic dream is that I'm the only waiter and the restaurant is, of course, packed. I go to one table and they want a will drawn up, another table wants their lunch, everybody is screaming at me, and then out of nowhere a guy comes up and says, "Dude, you've got a physics final *now*, and if you don't pass it you're not going to graduate from college!" And I tell the guy, "No, I dropped that class the first week," and the guy says, "The professor doesn't know that," and suddenly I'm in a physics lab. Then I wake up and I think, "I hate my job."

Dan Shapero
San Francisco, California

I'm sure there have been nights where you have sprung up in bed in a cold sweat and said, "Holy shit, man, I can't take one more table!" Everybody has, right? I've probably had five nightmares that I can remember. My worst one was when I was working in a Mexican restaurant in Austin. I dreamt I was the only waiter on the floor and the whole restaurant filled up. And the waiter dreams never end happily. In this dream I was waiting on the governor, at the time it was Mark White, and he was in having lunch. I don't remember the exact details of the dream but I think it's safe to say that I made his afternoon hell.

Dickie Mallison
MacArthur Park
San Francisco, California

I have nightmares almost every night. I dream that I'm in my bed in boxers and a T-shirt and I still have to take care of a table but I can't, or that it's 4:00 A.M. and people keep arriving to eat and I have to serve them. The sun starts to come up and the customers from the next day start to arrive and I can't get home to sleep. The worst one is that I will dream that my bed is somewhere in the restaurant and I can't get to sleep

because people keep passing by and wanting things—
and I can't get out of bed because I don't have any
shoes.

Dimitri Rathschech
New York City

At Legal Seafoods in Boston we used to call them
Scrodmares. Scrod is the cheapest kind of fish. We
called them Scrodmares because we all had them.
When you work eight hours straight like that and
you're *so* busy, it's unavoidable. I mean, you can drink
yourself into unconsciousness but right before you
wake up you'll be waiting tables. In the typical dream
you always have an incredibly large station. You know,
you're waiting on Candlestick Park or something. Mine
are always like that. Some people have them where it's
snowing, or they have to climb a hill to get their food, I
just always have a *huge* station. There are no acts of
God or strange calamities in the weather or anything,
it's just me waiting on twenty thousand people.

Garrett Harker
San Francisco, California

I have a recurring dream that I'm dropped in the
middle of a rush, and it's that kind of dream where
you can't move no matter how hard you try. Of course
I'm the only waiter, all the tables want their food,
nothing is coming out, and I don't know what to do.
It's terrifying. It's like a roomful of people hate you
and you have to stay there. And it's interesting because the geography of the restaurant is always different; one night it's a Swiss chalet, the next it's a
warehouse. I think it's a sign that I need to get out of
this line of work.

Gregg Ostrin
Beverly Hills, California

When I'm starting at a new restaurant I'll usually
get nightmares. You can wait tables forever and you

still get anxious at a new job. It's not like there's a universal place for the straws, you know? So the first night you work you get in the weeds. And since you're starting a new job you're broke, so you have to work the next night. Because who with money would try to get a job waiting tables? So you go home after the first night, go to bed, and wait tables all night long. And then you get up and go wait tables. You just wait tables for about a week solid. For me the dreams are usually the totally-in-the-weeds variety. Or worse yet, there is nobody in the restaurant and I'm still in the weeds. You know those dreams where you're running away from somebody but there is something in your eyes? It's like that. I'll be trying to get these two drinks for this one table and I can't get them. And I know in the dream that I shouldn't be in the weeds, that I only have to get these two drinks. It's really stressful.

Waiter X
Khin Khao
New York City

I had this nightmare a while ago where the restaurant was full, I was the only one there, and I was moving really slow. And I couldn't move any faster. Then all of a sudden I was wearing a bikini and I couldn't get to my clothes. It was horrible. I needed to get to all these people, I had to get water, I had a million things in my head. Then the dream shifted; something else happened and I was in the hills of Switzerland. Then in the middle of this dream in this bucolic setting I was like, "Shit! Those people are still waiting for water!" I had to go with this silver pitcher to this mountain stream and fill it up with water and run back to the restaurant where all these people were furious and wanted to kill me.

Jennifer
L'acajou
New York City

I just had a nightmare the other night. In the dream I had food to deliver and I was somewhere very far away, and I wasn't going to be able to get back to deliver the food. But this one was good because *I didn't care.* So maybe if dreams are true it won't be much longer, maybe I will get out of having to do this for a living. Most of the times the dreams are so bad I have to wake myself up.

Michael K.
The Grill
Beverly Hills, California

I recently had a dream that the entire waitstaff was seated in my section and I was their waiter. In the dream they were all screaming at me.

Naiem Mohammed
Museum Cafe
New York City

I constantly have waiter's nightmares. Generally I will be in a restaurant space and it will be about two thousand times the size it really is. And every table has been seated, every table has a menu, and I'm the only waiter. There have been times that I'm the only waiter and I'm naked. Then I've had the dream where I walk into the dining room and everybody is waiting to sit down and none of the tables are set; no cloth, no napkins, nothing. The dreams never end well and I always wake up in a cold sweat.

Ray Proscia
Georgia
West Hollywood, California

I have had several nightmares where I am the only person running the place. I'm cooking, I'm the hostess, I'm bartending, and I'm waiting tables. Another dream I have had is that I'm trying to com-municate with a customer and nothing is coming out

of my mouth so I have to act everything out with cha-
rades.

Robin Maynor
Linn's Fruit Bin
Cambria, California

I usually have nightmares after a double when I have
to work brunch the next day. And then it's like you never
left. You start thinking that you might as well work in a
twenty-four-hour joint, because that's what it feels like
you're doing. My usual dream is that I'm naked. Or I'm in
the restaurant in my tie and vest but I couldn't find my
pants. And I can't figure out how I got there like that.
I mean I don't feel great about what we have to wear
anyway; I feel like a eunuch. And I have to wait on these
big-breasted, beautiful women, and I'm feeling like a
schlubb. It's the worst thing in the world. So in my
dream I walk out in my vest, my tie, and my sneakers,
and all my nightmare customers come in. I've had this
dream three times. They don't notice that I don't have
any pants, and I'm totally in the weeds, and I can't figure
out why they don't notice that I'm half naked. It's just really, really awful.

Robin Shipley
Granita
Malibu, California

I once dreamt I was sitting in a TV and driving it and
I ran into a customer's car. I very seldom get time for TV.

Rose Larsen
Rose's Den at the Boulder Inn
Milepost 28, Highway 93
Kingman, Arizona

I had a dream the other night. I had gone away for
two weeks and the first night I got back it was really
busy. I got home at midnight and went to sleep but I kept
waking up. At one point I woke up and it was 3:00 A.M.
When I fell back asleep I dreamt it was 3:00 A.M. and ta-

bles were still coming in and I thought, what is the deal? It's 3:00 A.M. and people are still coming to eat. In my dream my bed was in the back of the restaurant and every time I would fall asleep another table would come in and wake me up. It was bad.

Ryan Delmar
Del's Pizzeria
Pismo Beach, California

Waiting

At four o'clock this afternoon I will walk the five blocks to Jethro's Bar & Grill and begin my shift. I will set up the dining room, fill the ketchup bottles and salt and pepper shakers, cut bread, prep the coffee station, and do all the other mindless tasks that must be done by a waiter before a restaurant opens its doors.

At five o'clock I will sit down to the staff dinner—the best part of my workday. The cooks prepare a meal, the waiters set the table and serve the food, and we all sit down together for thirty minutes to eat and talk. I love the people I work with; they are a warm, overeducated, fascinating group of people. The entire staff can talk knowledgeably about art, theater, dance, politics, and the most intimate details of their coworkers' personal lives. It is never dull.

After dinner I will clear and reset the table, dim the lights, and serve food from 6:00 P.M. until 12:00 A.M. We will wait for the last table to leave, do our closing duties, split up the tips, and walk out the front door. I will get home between 1:00 A.M. and 2:00 A.M.

I am thirty-four years old as I write this chapter. I will be thirty-five when this book comes out. If you had told me twenty years ago that I would be waiting tables when I was thirty-five, I would have laughed in your face. Then I would have slit my wrists. It's probably a good thing that we can't see the future. I think our ability to adapt to life's harsher realities is contingent upon them being presented in a haphazard, day-to-day fashion.

It may surprise you to learn that I didn't always want to be a waiter. I didn't study Pre Serve in college or anything like that. Since I was five years old I have known that I wanted to be a musician. Actually, at that age I wanted to be *in* Herman's Hermits. *Herman's Hermits On Tour* was the first record my father gave me, and I remember listening to it over and over, fantasizing that it was me singing those songs. Eventually I learned to play guitar and sing, but being a musician is not a realistic career goal for a kid in Stillwater, Oklahoma. They don't teach courses in how to be a recording artist at C.E. Donart High School. Or at least they didn't in the early 1970s. So I told my parents that I wanted to be a lawyer because that seemed to make them happy. I was a good student. I went to college in Austin, Texas, studied government, played in a band, and waited tables. Our band got somewhat famous regionally, recorded some records, and moved to New York. I got a job waiting tables here to help make ends meet.

After a few years of touring and fighting our band broke up. The rest of the band moved back to Texas, but I stayed in New York and waited tables. I put a new band together and we got signed to A&M records. I quit waiting tables. Our record came out and died; the band broke up. I waited tables. I wait tables. I am a waiter. I wait.

People do this job for a variety of reasons. For me it is a way to have a flexible schedule, keep my days free, and make just enough money to get by. As far as those things go, it has worked to my advantage. I really do spend my days writing songs or writing this book. If I show up at work tired, so be it. When I have had the opportunity to go on tour, or drive around for weeks interviewing waiters and waitresses, I have covered my shifts and gone. But as far as the actual work goes, waiting tables does not fulfill me in any way. I love the people I work with, I like many of the people I wait on, but when I think about it, I hate my job. I know that some people truly love waiting tables, but it is hard for me to believe that anyone could feel about it the way I feel about music—that it is a part of who I am, and that I can't imagine a life without it.

I go through periods where I feel like a failure. I don't like the notion that I am a thirty-four-year-old waiter. If anyone asks me what I do for a living I will tell them, but I am not proud of it. My brother-in-law once said that he admired me because I was the only one of his friends who had stayed true to his ideals and followed the dreams of his youth. It sounded very heroic. But I don't feel like a hero when someone is yelling at me because the chef cooked their meat a little too much. I can't believe that it is my job to pretend to care about something so utterly insignificant. There are worse jobs, I know that. I wouldn't want to be a coal miner, for instance, or the guy who inspects the finish on outboard motors to make sure the paint hasn't run. It's all about expectations. I expected—and expect—great things from myself.

I have a new band. The players are great, the songs are great, we're starting to get written up, and the record companies are sniffing around. We could get signed tomorrow. If that happens, I will be able to quit my job—if only for as long as it takes to record an album. There are no guarantees in show business, you get to learn that lesson again and again.

Every so often I take stock of my life. I tell myself that this is the life I have chosen, and ask myself how much longer I can live this way. I don't know the answer to that question. I'm not ready to give up yet. I consider myself lucky. I have always known what I want to do with my life, always had a vocation. Some people go through life looking. But I worry about the future. I don't have a pension. I can't afford health insurance. I don't know what would happen if I had an accident or became seriously ill. And I'm not getting any younger. When I work a Friday or Saturday night I wake up tired and sore the next day.

I'm an optimistic pessimist. I believe that everything is going to go wrong but that I will be okay in the end. I guess you call that faith. And faith is all we really have. Waiting tables has taught me many things. I have learned about manners, grace, and patience. It has humbled me more than I needed. More than anything, it has shown me how much I really do believe in myself. I could not go to work tonight if I didn't think that I had the talent to be a successful singer and songwriter. It would be too much to bear.

Can I do this for another year? No. I'm not sure I can get through tonight. We'll see.

The first thing I asked the men and women whom I interviewed was what they wanted to do with their lives, and how waiting tables fit into the picture. I found out that, like me, most of the people had given it a lot of thought.

I was a waiter in college, so I did that for four years. In college it's a great way to make money—it's the most flexible job, so it's perfect. Then when I graduated I worked for an entertainment company for three years. I started writing for them and then I studied acting to help with the writing. After a while the acting became more important so I quit that job to study acting more seriously. At that time I started catering and then got a job in a restaurant. It was the most convenient thing to do, and it worked out really well. But now I'm not acting anymore. There were parts of it that I love, but ultimately it's not for me. I'm just not into it. But I did write a play and we performed it last year. We're going to do it this year again. So there is nothing like the flexibility you have with a waiter job. I'm starting my own business now and the job is ideal for that. I work late at night, from eight or nine o'clock until about three in the morning. Our restaurant, Cafe Luna, is open really late. It's not a typical waiter job; I can wear whatever I want to work. It's really down-to-earth. It makes it really tolerable. I don't know how well I would do in an uptight restaurant situation with typical, anal restaurant management.

I don't have an ego attached to my work and I think that is what makes me a really good waiter. If you have an ego in a restaurant it is a really bad thing because you have to tolerate such bullshit. I make really good money, better money than some of my friends who have these corporate jobs. I also have the ability to leave for three weeks and go on vacation or work on this business I'm starting. So I don't attach a negative stigma to my job right now. I mean, I'm twenty-nine years old and I'd love to not be waiting tables when I'm thirty, but if I have to it's okay. I'm trying not to build that up into something big because that's just self-defeating. It really is. I work with people who are older than me, not many, but there are a couple of people who are older than me, and it's not a big deal. Nobody makes a big deal about it. I just landed in a great situation with this restaurant. You can go in there in a bad mood and it brings you right up. We yell, we make noise, it's just that kind of atmosphere. If I were at a different place I might hate it. I guess I'm a little spoiled that way right now.

Tom Andonian
Los Angeles, California

I wait tables because I can handle people. It's good money, the tips are good, and it's the best job that I can find right now. What do I want to do with the rest of my life? I would love to do something with music; I play guitar and sing and stuff, but I don't know what. I don't know what kind of future that holds, as far as paying the bills is concerned. I've been doing solo stuff, just me and the acoustic guitar. I play at a coffee shop sometimes, and tomorrow I'm making a five-song demo tape. But I don't know if I'd ever leave here to go to Los Angeles or anything. I like it here, I love the ocean and the air, it's fun.

Ryan Delmar
Del's Pizzeria
Pismo Beach, California

Waiting tables you're not going to get anything but cash in your pocket—there's no ladder to climb. And the money can never be good enough. Everyone has to take a break; I worked at Benny's for two and a half years, and finally I just went down to New Orleans for a while to chill. I mean, I met a lot of people through Benny's. My friend Sara calls me the Mayor. I know everybody on the street. I ran into seven people in New Orleans who knew me from that restaurant. I had never been to New Orleans in my life. But you have to take a break every now and then. I've worked in restaurants where I hated it so much that I would go in the walk-in and cry. Or cry on the way to work. I told a friend of mine at Melrose and he said, "You cry, too?" No job is worth crying over. Screw it. Starve for a while.

Russell Dean Anderson
Miracle Grill
New York City

I love being a waitperson. I'm sixty-eight years old so I guess I'll be doing it for the rest of my life.

Rose Larsen
Rose's Den at the Boulder Inn
Milepost 28, Highway 93
Kingman, Arizona

I work at Granita, it's one of Wolfgang Puck's restaurants. Like any other profession there are different levels, and this is the elite level. If you can become a waiter at one of his restaurants, it means you've made it. But then you're like, yeah, okay, how much longer do I have to be here? I was fortunate because when I was in New York I became friendly with some chefs. And the chef for the last restaurant I worked at in New York came out here to be the head chef at Wolfgang's new restaurant.

The restaurant has this underwater motif. It's near the beach, but there is no view of the water; so Wolfgang's wife, who decorated the place, commissioned about fifty artists to do different pieces. The floor is done in this incredible terra-cotta tile. It's just gorgeous. Everything was hand-laid. So we were there when the restaurant was opening placing seashells with glue, and having to sleep there to guard it.

This job is my bread and butter. It's the most flexible thing, and they're really good about giving me time off when I need it. I am an actress and a comedienne. I do stand-up and sketch comedy and that sort of thing. And that's why I moved out to Los Angeles. It was definitely a good move. I got out of an abusive relationship and career-wise there is so much more out here. In New York you really have to look to find things, and here it's right in front of your face.

Having come from New York is also a plus out here. I think people take you a little more seriously. It gives me an edge, and I think I'm a lot more savvy than many of the people out here. It gives you more soul, which is something that is lacking in Los Angeles.

I think it is very helpful to work in the kind of restaurant I work in, because I wait on the big powers-that-be in the business. On the other hand I think they do start to think of you as a waitress. But eventually, if they're good people, they start to care about you. I mean, I've gotten auditions from it, and a lot of interviews and that kind of thing. I got an agent from it, too. So I think that it has been a good thing that way.

Robin Shipley
Granita
Malibu, California

I don't know what I want to do with my life, and waiting tables just pays the rent, basically. One of my least favorite questions when I'm working in a restaurant is— you'll get some people from the Midwest, and they're charmed by the restaurant, and they're charmed by you because you're a New York chick—and they go, "So what are you? Are you an artist or a singer?" and you go, "I'm a waitress." First of all, why discuss it with people? And second of all, isn't it enough to be a waitress? I mean, I know it's kind of sad, but it pays the rent. I could never work a nine-to-five job, it would drive me nuts. You make more money waiting tables and it buys you time. It's more flexible, so if you have little projects you're working on you can do them.

I started doing it because I was really in debt and I needed to make cash. I stopped working retail and started working in restaurants. It wasn't until recently, like in the past couple of years, that I even thought I could sing. I would always sing with the radio and whatever, and then I thought, well maybe I could do that. I mean, there are people who are worse than me. It's a real hard thing though, I go through periods of being confident about it, and then not. It gets depressing; it's like, oh my God, I'm just a waitress, I'm not doing anything else. That's the point when it's really like, okay, I have to do something now. I look in the want-ads and think, isn't there an interesting job that I could do, even though I have no skills? What I studied in college, anthropology, has nothing to do with anything—I just loved it. I just took classes in what I liked. I mean, what is college for? It's an education, right? I never saw it as a stepping-stone to a career like a lot of people do. That's probably why I'm a waitress now. But if other things in your life are okay, it's all right. I'd rather be how I am than work at a gross office job and go to lunch with weird women and meet at the Hourglass. I'd rather be me than do that.

See, I haven't really found my niche yet, so I'm not sure what it is, specifically. I love what Sandra Bernhard does, how it's like, a bunch of things. I don't really write songs; I like to sing other people's songs. Talk about having no musical integrity. But I think I'm funny, too, so I should be able to work that into the act. I think I'm funny—I just said that. Oh my God, I'm cursed. When you're waiting tables it's kind of depressing, so you have to go okay, these are my talents, and this is what I have to do with them, because I can't do this for the rest of my life—there is no way. I don't want to be sixty years old and popping gum, you know, and my name will be Flo by then, or something, and I'll have a bouffant hairdo. Have you ever gone to an old diner, and there are old waitresses like that, and you always wonder: Did they have goals that never came through? You know what I mean? Were they Rockettes, or whatever? That's the downside. You can't really think about that.

I had some really demented idea in my head that I was going to get discovered. Everybody does at a certain point. I started at it so late. It's really easy to lose faith sometimes, but I have to believe that I'm going to do this. I have to, to get through my day, and my job and everything. Sometimes all you can do is live hand-to-mouth. There have been so many financial setbacks in my life recently that I haven't been able to plan very far ahead. At this point I don't really have a plan.

Rebecca Hall
Hourglass Tavern
New York City

I was going to be a waitress until I decided what I was going to be. All of a sudden it was ten years later and I thought, gee, now I'm pretty good at this. So I still don't know what I want to be when I grow up. I've done everything there is; I've gone to airline flight-attendant school, real estate school, and taken cake decorating classes. I've taken every kind of course I thought I would like, and I never liked it. I went to college, no big deal. I was going to be a dental hygienist, too. But then I thought, do I really want to work in somebody's mouth? So I started at a fast-food restaurant in Vegas. I worked for this guy who was really great, and he taught me the basics of what I know. It was all about getting everyone in, feeding them, making them happy, and restocking before the next rush. It was such a challenge, and very rewarding. I liked meeting all the people, I liked the instant gratification, and I was good.

I don't think I could sit behind a desk. I like the movement, I like the selling. I actually see myself as a salesperson, that's what I can really do. I was waiting on a guy who owned a Cadillac dealership and I was selling him a piece of cake and he said, "You should be selling Cadillacs!"

Growing up in Vegas I worked at lots of hotels. Now I want to work at a place for a long time. I don't want to work here and there, and here and there. My sister and brother have had one or two jobs in their whole life, and I've had maybe thirty. And that was just in Vegas. Then I moved to Florida and I had twelve in one year. That's one a month. It was crazy. It took me three years to find a good job, and then I stayed there for four years. And then I moved here.

I have no idea what the future holds. I worked at Denny's in Boca Raton, the busiest one on the East Coast. I worked with a woman who had had seven careers; she's a nurse, she's a real estate agent, she's an accountant, she had done it all. I said, "What are you doing waiting tables?" and she told me, "You make better money doing this." It was really discouraging. I was going to college and it made me want to drop out. I mean, you go to four years of college today and you get out and there are no jobs. People ask me if I want to do this until I'm fifty, and I say that it depends on your outlook. I enjoy this. I happen to be very good. I truly believe that if you don't enjoy what you do, get out tomorrow. Get out today. But I actually enjoy it.

Becky Milici
Fama
Santa Monica, California

I wait tables because it is easy for me to get a job doing it. I have experience. And ideally, I can make a lot of money. Right now I'm not making a lot of money because

I'm working at a new restaurant, but I'm doing fine, you know what I mean? I just moved to New York, so I'm getting some New York experience and learning about finer dining. And although I'm definitely burning out fast, working in restaurants is what I need to do right now to earn a living.

As I said, I just moved to New York a couple of months ago from Boston. I studied film production there at Boston University. When I arrived here I immediately got a job waiting tables, but I also work part-time at Miramax films. That's an interesting job, but I don't think I want to be on the production side, the technical side, anymore. I'm not sure what I want to do now, but I think it will have something to do with writing or photography. It just depends on what comes up. I don't really want to work at a company like Miramax for the next ten years either; it sounds so unfulfilling. The business side just isn't interesting to me. Except maybe acquisitions.

What will I be doing in ten years? I think I'll be working in film or photography. I might get my master's in photography. I don't really feel like I'm trained for anything now. Except for waitressing. But I don't want to do that forever. I'll just do it until I have a steady income from something else.

Kelsey Geisler
Trompe L'oeil
New York City

I work at Georgia, a southern-food restaurant, which is about six months old. It is considered one of the hot restaurants at the moment. There are a lot of celebrities, and it's fun.

Waiting tables is a lot like being on stage. You wear a costume, and it's all about presentation and show. I really love the restaurant business. I'm really lucky because I think I'm one of the few who really enjoys working in a restaurant. I'm getting too old, so it's beating me up physically, but I love the work. I've been doing this now for seventeen years, which is half my life.

I had been considering giving up my acting career in New York and one of my mentors said, "You've never been to Los Angeles, why don't you go out there and see if something happens out there for you?" And New York made it really easy for me to leave. It had become an ugly place to live, and I didn't like the people. I landed here and I fell in love with it. I just love being here. The lifestyle, the sun, the weather, the people. And I'm *from* New York. I was born and raised there.

I haven't really got that much work out here yet. I've done one show, a stage show, and I hope to do another one soon. I really haven't had much success at all. I can't even get arrested. And I've tried.

> Ray Proscia
> Georgia
> West Hollywood, California

I've been waiting tables for two years, here and at other places. During the year I mostly go to school, and I wait tables during the summer. I'm a waiter by summer. This is a money thing for me, it's an easy way to make money. I study political science at SUNY Buffalo, but my whole family is in the restaurant business so I have a funny feeling that I'm going to end up in it, too. Hopefully, I'll get out and have an office job, nine to five, and I won't have to worry about it.

> Pietro Bottero
> The Dock
> Fire Island, New York

I still believe I will have a career as an actor. Waiting tables is just putting bread on the table. I think I have learned a lot from waiting; I learned how to wait tables, which wasn't such an easy thing to do. But it doesn't occupy an important place in my life. I don't like to say that I'm a waiter. I'm unhappy that I'm a waiter. But that's what's good about the job I have now. I don't dread going in, it doesn't bother me, it's pretty easy. So it doesn't stay with me all day long; I can go in and out. And I'm really good at it now.

I made the core of my friends at this one restaurant in New York called Pesca, so I'm really grateful for that. It was a really great time, and most of my closest friends are from that time. But that's not an issue for me now, because I have all these great friends.

I would hate to think that the only thing I really knew how to do in my life was work in a restaurant, although I could do that if I wanted to. I learned how to cook from spending so much time in the kitchen, and of course that's a great thing.

I'm going to my twenty-fifth high school reunion, and that's really hard for me. I almost decided not to go, but I think I will after all. I'm really embarrassed that I'm a waiter, and I'm sorry to say that. I'm not ashamed of the person I am, but I just feel like I haven't accomplished that much.

Michael K.
The Grill
Beverly Hills, California

Waiting tables gives you a lot of freedom to decide what you want to do. I was not one of these people who had a fire in the belly to save the world, or be a politician, or be a doctor, and when I dropped out of school the first time I got a job as a waiter because I wanted to. I thought I could make good money and spend time finding out what I wanted to do. And it's worked out that way. I've met a lot of different people and been exposed to a lot of different things. I've been able to figure out what I want to do and also let things fall into my lap. You know, everybody, at one time or another, walks into a restaurant. I met Cameron, this woman who had me write an article for her magazine, in my restaurant. Shit like that happens.

I got my first job when I was twenty or twenty-one,

and I'm thirty-three now, so that's what, twelve years? I'm not tired of it yet. If I wanted to I could be the manager of a Manhattan restaurant right now, and it wouldn't be that hard, if I wanted to politic and network, to own some place, or own a part of some place. But it's hard for a restaurant to make money, and the minute it starts to make money you have to start planning how to get out of it, because it's not going to make money forever—at least in this town. So I really don't want to be in the upper end of it.

Since I moved to New York I have gone back to school and decided that an academic thing is a major option, and that I would like to write more. School and writing are intellectual things; they are emotional things, too, but you are in your head sitting at a desk, so it's good to have to go into the restaurant at four o'clock and bust your butt, use your wits, and use your body. The essence of this work is staying hooked up with everybody—the customers, the manager, the other waiters, the kitchen staff; I like to balance that with sitting and reading by myself, or writing.

As I have gotten older I have finally come to the point where I think I have something to write about. It's been a really long process. There are people like Truman Capote and Tennessee Williams, who came out of the gate gangbusters and were writing at an incredibly young age, and then they petered out and their later work began to disintegrate. And then there are people like Don Delillo, who didn't start until he was forty and gets better every time. For me it has taken a long time to allow myself to think that I might have something to say. And the steps to that were walking away from anything like it and slinging hash, and hustling drinks, then going back to school and studying literature, then taking my first writing course, and so on. I had opportunities to write before and didn't take them. It seems to me I took all the steps I had to, and took them as slowly as I had to, and the reason I was able to do that is that I was waiting tables. It fed me with a lot of material and didn't tax the part of my brain that I needed for my other work.

I don't want to be a forty-five-year-old waiter. I just got my first article published. Yesterday when the magazine came in the mail I thought, okay, this is what I want to do and this is the next plan; I'll write an article about this and submit it to *Details*, and I'll try to get an assignment. All this stuff went through my head and it was making me anxious. I had to tell myself that I just got my first article published and that I should really dig it for the afternoon. So I took the magazine in to work and showed it to everybody.

Mark Collins
Universal Grill
New York City

I think waitpeople in general are living on the edge. I think they're right on that line of never getting it together. They make good money and they can sit back for a long time because they're making a good $500 a week. I've really been thinking about it this week for the first time, and I think I want to stay further and further away from people who are waiters. The ones who I do want to stay friends with are the ones who are thinking the same things as me. It's not a career. Not unless you're like forty-five years old and you've made a conscious decision—but I don't think anybody does. I don't think anybody says, "I'm going to be a waiter when I grow up." You don't do that. You do it because you're doing something else and you need a no-head job. That's why I got into it. I used to teach to make money but it took up too much of my time for preparation—and I wasn't getting paid enough. But when you wait tables you always have to keep your goals in mind. Especially when you're working in the four-star restaurants, because it's so easy to lose sight of them. For the first time I'm looking at myself and I'm looking at other waitpeople around me and I'm saying, "He's going to make it, he's not, she's going to make it, she's not." It's scary. I think I just want to make sure that I keep taking risks. Because being in a situation like that is risk-free. Except that there are occupational hazards—I mean you could get a bullet shot into you any late evening, and you could get cancer from all the smoke you inhale. You just have to make sure you're having an exciting life, and waiting tables just sucks that out of you.

Freeda Kaufman
Jethro's Bar & Grill
New York City

I definitely don't want to wait tables for the rest of my life. I started doing this when I was eighteen, and I promised myself that I would stop by the time that I was twenty-three, because if my career hadn't taken off by then, then I was a lizard. But my career took off and I still needed money. That was when I was in college, and shortly after that I dropped out of college and went to Paris for a while. I am a dancer, and when I went to Paris I told myself that if I didn't get a job dancing by the time I was nineteen that I was going to quit. It turns out that I got a job, but that was the most unrealistic expectation in the world. And I still get demoralized. I think, my God, I can't believe I'm still a waitress. I'm in a company now, and I do my own work, and I work freelance, and I think that in a good year between one-half and two-thirds of my income is generated by dancing; but it's a poverty-line existence without the waiting money. And it's a genteel poverty with the waiting money. I don't like waiting tables but it's a necessary evil. If I'm in a level mood it's fine—I work with people who I like for the most part, and one of the women I work with is a good pal. But the work itself can be humiliating. No matter how nice the people are, you're still serving them.

Jennifer
L'acajou
New York City

I wait tables to make money. It's the easiest job to make money quickly. I really don't know what I want to do with the rest of my life. I'm kind of experimenting with different things. I'm probably going to start school so I'll wait tables to get me through school.

Right after I graduated from high school I moved to New York City and started working as a waitress there. I became a workaholic. I worked doubles, and doubles, and doubles, made tons of money, and I loved it. I worked at a great place called the Beach Cafe. Then I decided I wanted to be an actress, so I moved to Los Angeles. I thought I would have no problem getting a restaurant job because I had nine years of experience, but it took me three months to get my first job here. Everyplace I went, they only wanted to hire men. I was told that the perception is that women talk too much and that people out here want a man who is just going to serve the food and leave.

I've worked at a couple of places out here. I worked at Corral Reef in Santa Monica for three or four months, and then I got a job in Beverly Hills working at a restaurant called Il Fornaio. It was hectic and fun there. The management was Italian, straight from Italy. They were very chauvinistic, but you get that in restaurants. The customers were great. You would get the Beverly Hills snobs, but the regulars were great.

I just lost my job there so I'm going to go work for my friend who is opening a new place. That will be great because I know her. She's tough, but she's fair.

Jackie Becke
Los Angeles

I'm sick and I'm applying for disability, which I qualify for, and the government hasn't come through with the goods so I'm back waiting tables a half shift a week. I really am fucked financially. I need money so I have picked up these shifts until I can straighten everything out. I'm not sure I really have the energy to do the work now. I haven't been working for the past four months and I just started back. I worked last Friday and it was okay; I was a little nauseous because of the cigarette smoke, but the next day I couldn't get out of bed until 1:30 in the afternoon. Normally I get eight hours of sleep and I get up and I'm fine. But the day after this shift I couldn't get out of bed and then when I did I was dragging around all day.

I have really great employers. They're letting me work one day a week because I can't make any money if I want to collect disability benefits. But I don't know what the government expects people to do. They tell you you can't make any money but it takes them six months to process the paperwork. I guess they just hope you'll die in the meantime. My boyfriend was helping to support me but he just doesn't make enough money. He's a waiter, too. But my restaurant really came through. They said they would tailor a schedule to my needs.

When I was working as a waiter/actor, before I was a waiter/actor/person with AIDS, my attitude was that I would just wait tables and take a class and somehow become famous because I am so talented. Now I'm much more focused. I have a business plan and I do a certain number of tasks every day. It's a business. You have to market yourself as an actor—decide how you want to represent your product, stay in contact with people, and network in any way that you can. That is why there are agents and casting people, because it's really hard to do this by yourself. And the ironic thing is that when you aren't a successful actor you have to do all this by yourself because nobody wants to see you. Now that I'm actually doing it I don't see how anybody waits tables and tries to be an actor. If I hadn't gotten AIDS I could never have become the wildly successful businessperson that I am *(laughs)*.

Waiter X
Khin Khao
New York City

I had always wanted to work as an actor, and I had been in acting school since I was thirteen, doing school plays and that kind of stuff. Then I went to USC in the Theater Program, and after that I moved to New York. When I got out of college I realized that nobody in theater school had told me how to get a job as an actor. So I started working for catering companies. I don't even remember how I got into that. But the catering was interesting because it was seasonal and you worked in all kinds of different places. You worked in people's homes, in museums—in New York everything is catered. And this guy I was catering with got me a job in a little restaurant on the Lower East Side, which turned out to be run by the Greek mafia. The guy who ran it had been a dancer in the '60s and had been in all these Broadway shows, but his mother had been a bag lady for the Greek mafia. And the rumor was that his mother had his father wacked. Nobody knew if it was really true or not. But these old Greek guys would always be sitting in the corner doing deals and they'd ask you to get them a cup of coffee and they'd give you a five. But at night the place turned into a gay bar. Of course everybody who worked there was gay except me. I was the only straight guy. It didn't faze me, it's just that when I started working nights I noticed that there were all these Leathermen around. And I started to learn how to wait tables.

The work really made sense in that I had my days free and the alternatives were not that great. I couldn't type so I wasn't going to do temp work in an office. I didn't want to proofread, which was another big career for aspiring actors at that time, so I just worked in restaurants all over New York. I had agents and I auditioned, and I did some off-off-Broadway theater and stuff like that, and I just kept doing it. I also moved back and forth across the country a few times. I moved to Minneapolis for a couple of years and worked in a big theater there. When I finally found myself back in Los Angeles this last time it just seemed natural to get another restaurant job. It becomes automatic. And I think that's one of the downsides of it. You know you can make money at it and there are always jobs out there.

Two years ago a friend of mine approached me and told me he was starting a theater company and that it was going to be composed of people who write their own material. When I was in Minneapolis I had edited and written for this mock gossip sheet for our theater company, so I had done a bit of writing. It was very easy for me to start writing and performing for this company. And I was very into it; I turned out a lot of material in a very short period of time.

I originally started to write so that I could act in my stuff. But I looked around and I saw that I've only had moderate success as an actor. I've always felt that I was a good actor; I always got plenty of encouragement from everybody from casting directors to teachers, but it got to the point when I hit thirty that I had to reassess. I had been doing it for ten years, I wasn't enjoying it, and the only place I was really doing any work was in class. I felt like a statistic. I felt like I was one more guy in Los Angeles who works in a restaurant and goes to auditions. And it seemed like more opportunities were happening for me as a writer. So I just said screw it, I'm going to write. And things are going well. I just got a literary agent. I wrote two scripts with a partner I went to college with, and our first one is actually going out today through the agent. Basically what has happened is that I feel that I'm on the road to something.

It's funny—being a writer you have much more control. I think the problem with acting is that you feel like you have no control over anything. The flip side is that I'm still waiting tables and I'm wondering if I should go do something else. My girlfriend's cousin is a very successful screenwriter and he says I should keep my restaurant job because it gives me the freedom I need. And it makes sense. So that's what I'm doing.

What's interesting about waiting tables in Los Angeles is that here the waiter is the lowest rung on the show business ladder. In other words, being a waiter in Los Angeles you are an appendage of the entertainment industry. It's true. I don't recommend it as a way to break in to show business, but where I work 90 percent of the people I wait on are in the business. They are agents, producers, lawyers, people there to make deals. *I* make deals. I've gotten scripts to agents and producers from just hustling them. Everybody's looking out for something.

The concept of the waiter has changed. It used to be if you worked as a waiter you worked as a waiter. You go someplace like the Russian Tea Room in New York and it's still that way. Those guys make $60,000 to $70,000 a year. They're waiters. But in most restaurants it's not that way. Most waiters, at least in New York and Los Angeles, are actors. Or they are trying to do something else. And as an actor I really romanticize about the old days. Actors used to drive cabs, dig ditches, work as clerks, or bank tellers—things that would make me open my veins after a week of doing. But it sure reads well.

Gregg Ostrin
Beverly Hills, California

It changes all the time, but what I want to do is basically performance. Some kind of comedy that I create that is entertaining. It's funny because I think that when my stand-up career takes off I'm still going to have to wait tables because that's where all my material comes from. On the other hand, I've had it with it; I'm really fed up.

I started waiting tables in 1980 or 1981, when I was living in Westchester County. I was going to college and needed a job and I knew that waiting tables was instant money. I started waiting tables in this place where I was the only guy and the only young person; everybody was like fifty or sixty years old—all these old ladies. That was probably the most argumentative staff I've ever worked with. All these old ladies had been waiting tables for forty years and it was ugly. They argued about everything: tables, seniority, cappuccino, salad bowls, anything. I was eighteen years old and making $80 a shift and I thought it was great. Then this old guy who I always waited on started bugging me to come work for him. He owned this bar in the Bronx, and I went to work for him as a bartender on the 9:00 A.M. to 5:00 P.M. shift. It was a busy bar in a German neighborhood. I was making $200 a shift serving Seagram's to old men and watching them pass out by noon. But it was like, fuck it, I'm making $200 a shift! From there I just kind of rolled. I was able to go anywhere. I lived in Bangkok for a while and worked at a restaurant in the Sheraton Hotel there. I found that I could pretty much travel anywhere I wanted and get work. And it also opened me up from being a shy, reserved kid to being exactly the opposite.

I don't think I can do this forever. I'm thirty-one years old and I'm really tired of waiting on these twenty-eight- and twenty-nine-year-olds who are successful. For instance, I wait on this woman all the time who writes for *Rolling Stone,* and she's a punk. She travels around the world all the time and gets driven around in cars. I don't want to get driven around in cars by any means, but it's a little tiring to be getting closer and closer to what I want and still be pressing shirts to wear to work. But I do see a time in the very near future when I won't have to do this any longer.

Gary Chiappa
Roettele A.G.
New York City

I started off as a busboy when I was seventeen, so I have been in the restaurant business for eleven years. Is there a time when I feel that I'll no longer be able to do this job? Yes. Tomorrow. I'm serious; I'm so sick of it, I hate it. I *despise* it. I have a real problem with being talked to like I'm an idiot; especially since I have a de-

gree from UCLA. These people treat me like I'm a peas-
ant who is walking up to their table asking for money.

I wait tables because like every actor/writer in Los
Angeles it gives me enough money so that I can do the
things I want to do—and I have my days free. And I really
do make the time to do what I came here to do. For instance, Touchstone has one of my screenplays right now
and are hopefully working on a package for two big actresses whom they are very excited about putting together in this project. But I'm still waiting to hear about
that, and I'm not quitting my waiting job until I *get* it.

> Doug V.
> Los Angeles, California

I'm a writer as well as a waiter. I just made a movie. I
wrote a film with a friend of mine who is a director; he
raised the money and directed it. So I'm just biding my
time, waiting for him to sell it. It's about a performance
artist who gets hooked on crack and dies. It's a comedy,
actually.

I wait on tables because it was a natural progression.
My parents had a restaurant, and when I came to New
York to go to film school I thought, what can I do to
make money? So I lied and said I had worked there. My
mother was a waitress so I thought I could do it, too.
That was fourteen years ago.

I'm at the point now where I don't think I can do it
anymore. It's really hard to go into the restaurant. Especially now that I have a film under my belt. It was very
difficult right after the initial shooting. I took a month
and a half off to make the film; we were down in the East
Village with a big film crew shooting every day, and then
I had to go back to work and put an apron on. I can still
remember walking up to my first table on that day and
saying, "May I get you a cocktail?" I didn't want to get
them a cocktail, I would rather they had got me one.

Right now I'm one of those guys who is biding his
time. I'm not pathetic; I'm not one of those people who,

unless they become a restaurant manager, they have nothing else going for them. There are people who I work with who say, "I'm an actor, I'm an actor," and I'm always thinking, "You said that ten years ago and you have no prospects—what's going to happen to you? It's time to think about restaurant management." Every restaurant I have worked at has asked me to be the manager, and I have refused every one. I figure once you're in there, that's it.

Ted LoRusso
Perretti's
New York City

I worked for four years at Catch of the Sea at Third Avenue and 71st Street, and now I've been at Positano, at Park Avenue and 20th, for eight years. I'm in New York Tuesday and Wednesday, and out here on Fire Island Thursday through Sunday. I work six days a week. I enjoy waiting tables; I think it is fascinating dealing with people. A lot of them are a pain in the ass, but that's fascinating, too. I don't want to do this for the rest of my life. I should move back to my country, Brazil, and I'll probably go back to being a math teacher, which is what I used to do. I lived in Switzerland before I came to the United States, but I couldn't stay there. I couldn't get a visa, and I couldn't get a job without a visa. I had a friend in New York, so I came to New York. It was not easy to get a job here at first, especially when you don't speak the language. In my case it was very hard. I had to start as a busboy, and then I went to waiter, and now I'm the manager here. I prefer to wait tables, you make more money. My purpose to be in America is to enjoy life, but to make money as well. I told my boss that at the end of the summer I would like to go back to being a waiter, because I really don't care for management politics. It's too much, I don't have time for it. But I really should go back to my country. Not soon, but in a couple of years. Brazil is a beautiful country if you have money. But I guess every country is beautiful if you have money.

Ademir Dasilva
Positano
New York City

I have my good days and I have my bad, but for the most part I should say that I absolutely hate waiting tables. The only reason I stay with it is because of the money—overall it averages out to be almost twice as much as working in a store or someplace like that. Being a waitress in the East Village is different from most places. It sort of allows a coldness, an aloofness, that people almost expect. But you have to draw the line; I have been told many times that I have quite an attitude, and I do, but it's only because I am fed up with waiting on anal-retentive, needy people. Obviously I am very bitter, and waiting tables has done this to me. I am sick of sizing people up for the tip they might leave. I am sick of seeing people's ugliest side and getting annoyed by it. I am endlessly sick of this business. I have to quit.

What to do with the rest of my life? Good question. I know waiting tables is not in my long-term plan. I think I want to work with children, either in therapy or in education. Maybe I can teach them how to be good restaurant customers.

Amy Packard
New York City

I came to the United States two years ago from Poland. I finished university in Poland; I am a physical therapist. But I didn't work my job in Poland because after school I went to the United States. I wanted to come, it was my dream. Always I wanted to see New York City. I thought, big city, nice people, Broadway. I was surprised. I imagined New York City like Broadway; tall buildings, many lights, very beautiful, with places to play music. I looked at Broadway and I saw so many poor people. But now I like, I like very much. I went on vacation one month ago, I make trip. I saw so many states in United States. I missed New York City. After two weeks I started to think about New York. I'm going to stay for five years, six years, we'll see; I don't want to make plans. I'm going to stay for now.

Teresa's is my first job in United States. When I started I was busgirl because I didn't speak English. My next position is waitress. I like job. I meet so many nice people. I like it. But I'm going to change because it's hard. Maybe a different restaurant. It was easy for start because of the Polish people. But now I don't think I have enough practice with English. We speak Polish in the restaurant.

It's hard because I'm always afraid my English is not good enough for the work I want to do. It's hard to leave the restaurant also, because I know people—I like these people. It's a long day. From six o'clock to four o'clock, ten hours. I work alone one hour. My friends come at seven o'clock—they start at seven o'clock. I like morning shift. I have time after work, I can do something. I can go out, but not too late. Sometimes I go out and I come home at five o'clock and it's time to go to work.

I like people. I always smile, so people, I think, like me. I have some customers I don't like. Most are nice. Nice people. I think waitress is a good job, but not for all life. For two or three years, but not for all life.

> Beata Brzozowska
> Teresa's Coffee Shop and
> Restaurant
> New York City

I wait tables strictly for money. And I do it with such an attitude that it's amazing that I haven't been fired more often than I have. I would have to say that I'm probably the worst waitress that I know. If I had waitresses like me when I went out I would never tip them. Actually, I take that back. When I go out to eat and I have bad waitresses I give them more money, because I see myself in them.

I think I can do this kind of work for about three more weeks. Which is convenient because I'm moving to California in three weeks to be a movie star. I hope that I don't have to wait tables out there. But it is the fastest way to make money. If I can find someplace in California that has a big movie industry clientele I might wait tables out there. But it's horrible. One of my biggest fears is being a waitress when I'm forty years old.

Shawna Mason
Lone Star Roadhouse
New York City

Right now I hate waiting tables. I go in and another personality takes over. I become sarcastic, I become bitchy—all in the name of humor. I could just tear somebody to shreds. And that's sort of how I get through the night. For a while it worked, and it was fine, and then I realized that it wasn't really a good thing because I was hurting people. So I tried to stop, and I was pretty successful at that, but now it's taking over again because it's just the way that I cope. And at the same time it's comfortable because it's not a risk. To put myself out on the line and do what I want to would take a risk. But I've been working in restaurants since I was sixteen, and I'm thirty-four now. I'm an artist; I do illustrations, and I'm good. I know I can do it, and I'm almost ready. But I think I've got to get real, real sick and tired of the restaurant to do it. Waiting tables is good money; I've been making a living at it for so many years and it's comfortable because I know what is expected of me. And it's a Peter Pan thing, too—growing up, you know? But it's the only thing that I can do to make the money that I make. And it's the only thing that I really know how to do, besides art. I think I can keep doing it for another year at the most.

Bob Dombroski
Orso
New York City

I live in Los Angeles and have lived here all my life. It's very important to be something here, or trying to be something. Well, I'm a waitress and I don't know what else I want to be yet. I'm not really worried about it right now. But it sure seems like other people are worried about it.

> Cara Green
> Swingers
> Los Angeles, California

Being a waitperson pays my rent and my student loans, which an entry-level position in my field won't do. It also seems to appeal to my sense of order, perhaps over-stimulating it a bit: preparing, delivering, speed, and precision. I graduated from NYU with a B.A. in international politics, German, Russian, and peace and global policy studies. Most jobs I want involve going overseas and are volunteer or require a master's degree. Short of ruling the world I'm having a problem getting a real job. I've applied to some American companies investing in Russia.

> Cherie Hamblin
> Moondance Diner
> New York City

I'm not sure what I want to do for the rest of my life, but I wait tables because I love the people in the restaurant business. They're my favorite kind of people. And the job itself allows you to do what you like best. It frees up your time so you can pursue something else, which for me right now is bicycle racing. I have the time I need to travel and hang out. Also, it's the easiest way to make fast money—you can go to any city in the United States and snag a job waiting tables. You can make a career out of it; I mean some people have. I can make as much money waiting tables working half the time as some people working a forty-hour-a-week office job.

> Dickie Mallison
> MacArthur Park
> San Francisco, California

The first part of what I want to do with my life is stop waiting tables. Waiting tables is a stepping-stone. It's the furthest into the real world that I'll go. I paint and I write, and eventually I want to be a filmmaker. Part of the reason I paint and write is that I can't afford camera equipment and I want to creatively express myself.

Waiting tables is easy cash and you get to take it home with you. There is, obviously, a lot of bullshit. The hardest part of waiting tables is waiting for the guests to get there so you can get it over with. There are some aspects to it that I enjoy. One of the guys I work with put it in an interesting perspective; he said to think of it as your store. Your section is your store, and you are the storekeeper. You have your supplies in the back, and you have to pay your rent; that's what the house gets. And for the first time I thought, this is my place, so I want everything to look nice. And it's nice to serve people.

I have a theater background; my father is a theater director. I was born in New York City and went to high school in St. Louis. My mom and dad divorced so I ended up in Missouri. Then I went to California to find success and realized it was all inside in the first place. Wouldn't you know, it was there the whole time. It was a trap; L.A. is a trap. So it took a couple of years to get out of Los Angeles. I was waiting tables there also, and it was okay. I worked at some cool places and some crappy places. I worked at Red Lobster, which was a downfall. I mean it was the nicest Red Lobster, but it was horrible.

The greatest satisfaction I have experienced in waiting tables is when I could let go. When I could say, I don't need this anymore. I used to get really upset at the customers, and my boss would be pissing me off, and I would forget that I am in control; I am the universe, I can create my own reality. The moment I realized that I actually started laughing. It was like, I remember now; I remember who I am, hey, I don't need you, the universe has always taken care of me, so why get upset?

But one of the things that makes me upset is when I start to sound like a robot. Hi, my name is Dave and I'll be your server, this is the special, it's this, it's that, da dee, da doo, da da, this whole big routine. So I started doing these really bad jokes. And they laugh every single time. And if they don't laugh, I tell them it's a bad joke and they think that's funny. And I've done that over and over, and there are times that it really makes me sick because I'll leave the table thinking, God, I'm so fake. I hate that fakeness. I just want to say, "Have the tenderloin, it's excellent. Don't tell me you want it this way and that way, you're wrong. *I know.*" The customer is always right? Nah, the customer is always right because they're paying you, because they're giving you the money.

But there is a service aspect to it as well. I was raised with no particular religion, but to love thy neighbor and serve, and peace and harmony; I'm a '60s baby. So there is that aspect of it.

I came out to Santa Fe about a year and a half ago. It is starting, I can see the dream happening. The neat thing is that I realized the things I want to do, the writing, the painting, I can do anywhere. Once you find the success inside yourself, you can do that anywhere. So why not live someplace that is beautiful?

There are some joys to waiting tables. Some people who I waited on last week said, "Come to Pittsburgh, stay with us," and I don't know these people. I tell those people that if every guest was like them this job would be a dream. I mean, there are so many people who go on vacation and bitch and moan, bitch and moan. But there are people who say, "What's good, what do you like?" and they're into it. And some of those people don't leave a lot of money, but the fact that they're enjoying themselves makes it worth it. I got my stuff hanging in a gallery because of these two guys I kept waiting on. They said, "Dave, what do you do?" and I said I paint. They said, "We work in a gallery, we're having a show and we think your stuff would go great," and now they represent me. It just happened to fall out like that.

The Anastasi is one of the nicest places I've ever worked. They don't call us employees, they call us associates. Just that little name change makes a big difference. They care about us. For their first anniversary they had an employee art show. My food and beverage director bought one of my pieces, which was sweet. Two hundred bucks, thank you very much.

I suppose if I sat home and just painted I would be very happy, but there would be times that I'd be very lonely. It is a nice people thing. I realized I needed that when I took an office job for a year. I was making $10 an hour with no taxes, so it was sweet. My mother was the executive director of this dance company and she needed an administrative assistant, so my mom was basically my boss. So it was like, "Mom, I think I could go home and do this mailing list a lot better." So I'd go home, relax, watch TV, and fold and stuff three thousand envelopes over a three-day period and make $300. It was cake. But there were times when I was sitting in the office in front of the computer for two hours and I'd be going, GET ME OUT OF HERE! At least with waiting tables you are moving around.

There are some professional waiters out there—I don't see how they do it. I'm not knocking them, I just have higher aspirations. I want to work for myself and not slop food, even though it is beautifully presented on fine china, served from the left, and cleared from the right.

David Brockett
Inn of the Anastasi
Santa Fe, New Mexico

When I was in high school I had a big anxiety attack. I didn't realize what it was. I almost dropped out of school; it was very traumatic. My mom was agoraphobic, so this kind of thing runs in my family. I was very upset. In the end I decided that there was no way I could go away to college. I got out of school and got a job doing retail and I hated it. Then I got a job in a Mexican restaurant and I did very well. Within a month I was promoted to cocktail waitress, which was a big deal at that restaurant. All the other waitresses were very envious. And of course, the money was good. I was making more money than most of the people I knew. At the time I didn't envision another kind of life for myself so I just kept doing it and doing it. Then I became frustrated. I realized that I am too intelligent to do this forever. Not that I look down upon it—I just knew that it wouldn't be enough. So I did go to college. I loved it. This was in Florida. Then I decided to move to New York.

My brother was living in New York, and sometimes working as an actor. I had always wanted to get involved in acting also, and since I had family in New York, I thought I would move up. I came up here and I really liked it. I got in with a great group of friends, mostly gay men, and for one reason or another I didn't pursue the acting thing. I would always find a reason not to take a class, or to not get pictures taken. So I just kept waiting tables. For some reason I took a vacation in Florida, and when I came back I had another big anxiety attack. I became very depressed, and I returned to Florida.

When I moved back to Florida it took a while to get comfortable with my life there. But after some time I found a job at a really great Mexican restaurant. I made some great friends, made a lot of money, and bought a car. It was nice. And then I thought I might go back to school. All of a sudden I realized that I didn't want to settle. I realized that I really wanted to try to be an actress, or work in the film business, or something like that. So I decided to come back to New York again. I had left the city because I was afraid, and I didn't want to feel conquered like that.

Now I'm back here in New York waiting tables. And I'm fine. I do it because it's easy for me, and I can come and go. I'm not afraid of it. But I know I can do more. I'm hoping I can find the confidence in myself to live the kind of life I want to live.

Stacey Jurewicz
Pescatore
New York City

I'm going back to school, so waiting tables is conducive to my schedule. I'm sure there is something else out there that I can do, but I didn't invest enough time and energy to figure out what it is so I ended up going back to waiting tables. I've waited tables before, and I vowed that I would never go back to doing it again. I was living in Los Angeles and working at a place called Adam's Ribs, and I was fired for serving my girlfriend, who was not yet twenty-one, alcohol. It was a fun job, but by the time I got fired I was sick of it. I was tired of dealing with the public in that manner.

I am now taking prerequisite courses so I can go to chiropractic college next year. It will take three and a half years to complete my studies, and no, I will not wait tables during that time. I have to focus—I can't deal with the drudgery of waiting tables when I have major stuff to study. Maybe a couple of nights a week here and there bartending, after my first year is over, but I have decided I won't wait tables anymore.

Dan Shapero
San Francisco, California

I had to write a bio for something—I can't remember what it was for, and I counted back how many years I had been in the food business because I like to joke around and say I'm a food service professional. I realized it's been twenty-three years. I got my first job when I was thirteen years old working behind a bakery counter. I couldn't have guessed then that I was going to be around food so much. It's fit into my life really well. It fits into an actor's life really well because you usually manage to charm your way into a schedule that's flexible and make people like you enough to be on your side as long as you'll come to bat for them when they go to bat for you. So it's fit into my life. I think it's taken over my life in times of financial problems, but it's the easiest thing to do. It's the easiest thing for me to do. The cash is hard to say no to. And I want to say one more thing; I think waitressing is an amazing skill to have. Having been a waitress since I was nineteen, which is sixteen, or seventeen years, I realize that it's a skill that I respect now. Not that I really want to make a career of it, and unfortunately I'm thirty-six years old and it seems like I have, but I don't hate myself because I do it anymore. It's real honest, hard-earned money, and sometimes that makes my day.

Cyndi Raftus
Hourglass Tavern
New York City

The Ten Commandments

1. Thou shalt not touch thy waiter or waitress.
2. Thou shalt not be late and expect thy waiter or waitress to get thou where thou art going on time.
3. Thou shalt not ask to enter the restaurant before it is open or linger after it is closed.
4. Thou shalt not let thy children run wild in the restaurant.
5. Thou shalt not drink to excess and become meaner than usual.
6. Thou shalt not place thy elbows on thy table so thy waiter or waitress cannot serve thou.
7. Thou shalt not ignore thy waiter or waitress when thy waiter or waitress is trying to take thy order.
8. Thou shalt not whistle, yell, or snap thy fingers to get thy waiter's or waitress's attention. Ever.
9. Thou shalt not complain frivolously, for sport, or because thy needs are not being met in thy real life.
10. Thou shalt not leave less than a 15 percent tip.

Glossary

a la carte—Commonly means that items on a menu are priced individually, not all included in the price of a meal.

arm service—Serving food and beverages without trays.

bad tip shuffle—When a table leaves a poor tip and exits the restaurant with unnatural haste.

bar—A room or area in a restaurant intended for serving drinks. A good place to locate the owner or manager.

bell, the—An instrument used by the kitchen to summon the waiters. Indicates that an order is ready to go out to the table or that the chef needs another drink. Can cause salivation or heart palpitations in some waiters.

boned—See *shafted*.

bread hog—A customer who repeatedly asks for more bread.

brunch—A weekend shift during which heavy breakfast food is served to crabby people with nothing in their refrigerators at lunchtime. See *hell*.

buffet—A self-service spread of food.

buried—See *in the weeds*.

bus—To remove items from a table.

bus box or bus tub—A plastic container used to carry dishes, glasses, and silverware.

busboy or busperson—A waiter's assistant; one who removes dirty dishes and resets tables in a restaurant. Also known as a *slave*.

camel—A customer who needs his or her glass refilled repeatedly.

carafe—A glass container used for serving water or wine.

check—A bill, the document presented to the guest.

check average—The average amount of sales a waiter generates per guest. Frequently used to dispense perks like a good schedule or a good station, or conversely, to make a waiter's life miserable.

chef—A person in charge of the entire kitchen or one of its departments (pastry chef, etc.). Also known as tyrant, despot, dictator, oppressor, strong man, and that-asshole-in-the-kitchen.

clear—To take items away from a table after customers have finished with them.

comp—To give something away, usually a drink or a dessert.

cooler—A smallish ice bucket used to chill wines.

cover—a: A guest or customer. b: A meal. For example: "I don't know how I'm going to pay my rent, we only did twenty-five covers tonight."

creamer—A container used to serve milk or cream.

crop dust—To break wind in the dining room, especially in another waiter's station.

cut—To get off early. Restaurants with large staffs will frequently cut waiters as the evening progresses and business slows down.

daily double—See *double tip*.

dead—When a restaurant has no business.

deuce—a: A table for two. b: A table of two. Also known as a *two-top*.

door whore—See *host*.

double—To work two shifts in a row.

double tip—When a customer doesn't notice the *grat* and tips again.

dupe—Duplicate. A copy of a check that a waiter will give to the kitchen to get a food order or to the bartender to get a drink order.

du jour—Literally means of the day, as in a special of the day. Some guests can actually pronounce this.

du soir—Of the night. Few guests can pronounce this. Actual pronunciation is "do swa," frequent mispronunciation is "do-swar." Pretentious French words on a menu provide continual enjoyment for the waitstaff. Guests also seem to have trouble with the word *salmon*. Some European guests cannot pronounce *Caesar*, which is surprising. While this salad was invented in Mexico, I understand there were a few Caesars down Italy way.

eighty-six (86)—To be out of an item. Also used to describe being fired. Has entered the popular lexicon with an additional meaning: to be killed.

expediter—A person who calls out the orders to the cooks and organizes the outgoing orders for the waiters or runners.

fire—An instruction, usually verbal, from the waitperson or runner to the chef which indicates that a particular course should be prepared. For example: "Table twenty-three has finished their appetizers, *fire* their entrees."

flatware—Table utensils.

french people—See *shafted* or *stiffed*.

garnish—A food item added to a drink or a plate of food to enhance the visual appeal of the item. Usually immediately removed by the guest and placed in the ashtray.

grat—To add the gratuity to a check, typically 15 to 20 percent.

gratuity—Money left to compensate a waiter for his or her services. Usually insufficient.

hell—Brunch.

host or hostess—A person who seats tables in a restaurant, typically in a random or chaotic fashion.

in the weeds—To be hopelessly behind.

leftover—See *special*.

liqueurs—Beverages made of liquor, sugar, and flavoring. Typically served after dinner. A big help in boosting check average.

liquor—Alcoholic beverages containing 2/5 or more pure alcohol. As gasoline is to the automobile, liquor is to the chef and manager.

live stock—Crudités, salads, etc., set on the tables without having been ordered.

livestock—the guests.

mise en place—French term for sidework, or getting one's station ready. Frequently used in pretentious restaurants.

monkey dish—a small dish, usually bowl-shaped, used for serving small amounts of vegetables. More recently used for serving all the things that guests insist on having "on the side."

neat—A beverage served pure, without ice.

off the books—Working for a restaurant for no pay. The benefit being that neither the waiter nor the restaurant pays taxes. Very common in New York.

on the door—To be scheduled as a host or hostess.

on the floor—To be scheduled as a waitperson.

on the rocks—A beverage served over ice.

on the side—Serving dressings or condiments separately from the food that they usually come on so that the guests can preserve the illusion that they are living a more healthy lifestyle.

peanut butter sandwich—A couple having an argument at a table. For example: "I've got a peanut butter sandwich on four, they're really going at it!"

pony—A small stem glass used to serve straight liquors and liqueurs.

pooling—Dividing the tips among the floorstaff.

portion control—the standard size of a food order, used to some degree by almost all restaurants.

real job—Any job other than waiting tables, especially a nine-to-five office job.

regular—A customer who comes in often. I once saw a T-shirt that said, "A regular is just a regular pain in the ass." Enough said.

rocks—Ice.

round-trip meal ticket—When a guest, because of illness or drunkenness, throws up in the restaurant they are said to have bought a round-trip meal ticket.

runner—A waitperson who brings the food from the kitchen to the table.

service—a: The occupation or function of serving. b: Useful labor that does not produce a tangible commodity. c: To add a tip to a check. See *grat*.

setup—a: A place setting. Usually includes silverware and napkin, but can include glasses and plates. b: To reset a table.

side dish—A supplemental dish, such as french fries or a green vegetable.

side towel—A (generally) white service cloth, used for wiping up spills or cleaning things.

sidework—All duties performed by waitstaff other than serving tables. The tasks the *other* waiters never do.

shafted—To have received a poor tip from a table. For example: "Oh, man, I gave table thirty-six great service and they *shafted* me."

skim, the—Nontaxable cash income for a restaurant. This income is created by disposing of a certain number of cash dinner checks. Without these checks there is no record of the sales.

slammed—When a restaurant or a particular station fills up all at once. For example: "We got *slammed* at eight o'clock, I was *buried*!"

slave—See *busboy*.

special—A meal made from ingredients that did not sell in the previous week. Usually offered at a premium price.

speed rack—The thigh-level shelf directly behind a bar where the cheap liquor is kept for easy access.

split—A small bottle of wine.

squatters—A party that sits at a table too long, depriving the waiter of income from the next party.

station—The tables assigned to a waiter or team of servers.

stiffed—To receive no tip from a table.

straight—Refers to an undiluted drink or a heterosexual waiter or guest.

straight up—Without ice, frequently chilled.

swamped—See *in the weeds*.

tip cup—A vessel used to hold the waiters' aggregate tips. Usually a coffee can. The tip cup is generally kept behind the bar.

tips—Money left to compensate a waiter for his services. Never enough.

turn over—To have a table leave and "turn over" the table to the next party.

turn tables—Refers to turning tables over. A waiter's ability to turn tables can be directly related to his or her income; the more guests you serve, the more money you make.

waiter's ass—An irritation between the buttocks, similar to diaper rash. Less common in waitresses. Also known as *the ass*.

waiter burnout—A condition caused by waiting tables for too many years. Symptoms include the inability to be nice (or even civil) to the guests, lingering depression, lethargy, misanthropy, and an overall sense of hopelessness. There is no known cure for this condition.